Bell Witch:
The Truth Exposed

By Camille Moffitt Nichols
With Chris and Walter Kirby
(Owners of the Bell Witch Cave and Farm)

Copyright © 2003 by Camille Moffitt Nichols
United States Library of Congress-in-Publication Data
May 1, 2003
Bell Witch: The Truth Exposed
By Camille Moffitt Nichols
Registration Number: TXu-1-100-681
All rights reserved. Written permission must be secured from the author to use or reproduce any part of this book, except for brief quotations in critical reviews or articles.
Printed in the United States of America
First Edition, 2007
Reprint, 2024
Photos are copyrighted by the Historic Bell Witch Cave Inc. and have been used in this book by permission.

Table Of Contents

Introduction
Foreword: A Glimpse Into The Past

Section I: Living On The World's Most Haunted Property
Chapter One: Entrusted With The Land ... And Its Truth 1
Chapter Two: Sounds Of Horror 4
Chapter Three: Eerie Photos 12
Chapter Four: Throwing Open The Gates Of Hell 16
Chapter Five: First Sightings 21

Section II: The Secrets Come To Light
Chapter Six: Discovery — Human Bones 27
Chapter Seven: Captured On Video 31
Chapter Eight: The Final Piece Of The Puzzle 35
Chapter Nine: New Light On Old Stories 39
Chapter Ten: Yes, There Is A 'Bell Witch' 45
Chapter Eleven: Living With 'It' Today 50
Chapter Twelve: Voices From The Past 55

Section III: Bells' Hell
Chapter Thirteen: The Arrival 57
Chapter Fourteen: The Spirit Speaks 62
Chapter Fifteen: Mimicking The Scriptures 68
Chapter Sixteen: A U.S. President And The Witch 70
Chapter Seventeen: The Witch And The Slaves 73
Chapter Eighteen: The Torment Of Betsy Bell 79
Chapter Nineteen: Lost Love 84
Chapter Twenty: The Good Witch 87
Chapter Twenty-One: Mysterious Death Of John Bell 89

Section IV: Skeletons In The Closet
Chapter Twenty-Two: The Author's Views 92
Chapter Twenty-Three: No One Wanted You To Know 96
Chapter Twenty-Four: Predictions Of The Bell Witch 98

*The truth is a thousand times
more riveting than the myth*

Introduction

Nestled in the backwoods of rural Tennessee just above the bank of the Red River, dwells what experts believe to be the most haunted spot in America: the Bell Witch Cave.

Known throughout the world for its paranormal potency the Bell Witch Cave has endured for centuries as the subject of homespun myth and folklore, passed on by word of mouth, and recorded in books, movies and songs.

But what is the truth behind the myth? Is the cave home to a nineteenth-century witch released from Hell to torture the family of John Bell hundreds of years ago, as the myth purports?

Or is this haunting something larger ... something far more sinister than past generations could have imagined?

First, it must be established that the supernatural force known as the "Bell Witch" is still somewhat active and upsets the people who live there today, just as it did the people living there in the 1800s. Many of the strange anomalies that were occurring two hundred years ago are still playing out. The compelling difference between yesterday and today is that now there is proof.

Through the use of twenty-first century, military-grade sensory equipment and the expertise of anthropologists, archaeologists, historians and leaders in the field of paranormal phenomena, there is documented evidence (supported by non-doctored photos) which not only establishes that supernatural forces are in fact there — it explains why.

This is the only book written with and endorsed by the Kirby family, owners of the Historic Bell Witch Cave and Farm. It is the only book that reveals the truth — and the truth is a thousand times more riveting than the myth.

*The force known as the Bell Witch is immense.
It is bold. It is terrifying and it is real ....*

Foreword

Sensational accounts of supernatural events, occurring on what is now known as the Bell Witch Cave and Farm, came to light thirteen years after John and Lucy Bell and their children established their farm on the land in 1804.

Since then, countless newspaper articles have been published around the world about these mysterious happenings. Make no mistake about it, the Bell Witch phenomenon has never been about mere menacing apprehensions allegedly witnessed by a few.

It's about violent physical attacks that have injured countless people and allegedly killed one man. It's about a disembodied voice that, at one period in time, routinely disrupted local church services, mimicking the voices of the pastors, brazenly mocking the Holy Scriptures.

These and other supernatural anomalies happening in and around the Bell Witch Cave and Farm have been witnessed by thousands of people over the course of two centuries.

The force known as the Bell Witch is immense. It is bold. It is terrifying and it is real.

In the 1800s, these strange events were documented the only way they could be; through eyewitness accounts and the subsequent testimonies of some of the region's most prominent citizens including doctors, lawyers and ministers — even the seventh President of the United States, Andrew Jackson, who went to the Bell farm to investigate the rumors and experienced his own encounter with the witch.

Jackson was rumored to have said of his experience, "I'd rather take on the whole of the British army than to face the wrath of the Bell Witch!"

But the cause of the haunting, until now, has remained a mystery.

Books written on the subject, several by members of the Bell family, speculate that a curse was cast upon the family by a neighbor, Kate Batts, after a business deal between her and John Bell turned sour; therefore, some accounts refer to the witch as Kate.

Astonishingly, no one considered that long before the Bell family made its trek from North Carolina to Tennessee the problem was already looming, deeply rooted in rural Robertson County — along the Red River (given its name the day it flowed red with blood spilled during fierce fighting between the Choctaw and Cherokee tribes). No one questioned why the land was considered cursed by those tribes, nor why they abandoned it before the White man ever cast his lot upon it.

New evidence verifies that the Bells did not bring about the evil that tortured them, which was ultimately blamed for the death of John Bell. They were simply unwitting intruders, victims of a powerful force that they could not understand.

It's amazing that early recorded accounts of the Bell Witch phenomenon barely mention the cave, postured on the farm just yards from the site of the old Bell home, because it is that which entombs the secret. The cave is the genesis of the Bell Witch.

A Glimpse Into the Past

Before we explore the dark side of the Bell Witch Cave, it's important to understand the magnitude of its horrendous reign.

What follows is a brief account of the torture of John Bell, as seen through the eyes of his son, Richard Williams Bell (called Williams) who kept a diary of events. Although his father was persecuted daily (and nightly) for years — literally until he was dead — this focuses only on a small portion of a single day of his life:

"Soon after the spirit began to speak, it vowed to kill my

father," Williams writes. It repeated the threat over and over for years, growing more agitated and abusive each day. Every word uttered to "Old Jack" (its nickname for John Bell) was a blast of unrelenting curses and threats.

Eventually, John began suffering mysterious attacks on his health, which included visible facial contortions. He felt as though a stick was lodged in his mouth horizontally cutting into both cheeks. His tongue swelled, he couldn't eat, and he quickly began to weaken. Soon, he no longer left the house alone.

One morning, John called Williams to accompany him to the hog pen.

"We had not gone far before one of his shoes was jerked off," Williams later recorded in his diary. "I replaced it on his foot, drawing the strings tight, tying a double hard knot. After going a few steps farther, the other shoe flew off. There was no way that I could tie them to make them hold, notwithstanding his shoes fitted close and were a little hard to put on and we were walking over a smooth dry road."

This shoe-jerking continued all the way to the hog pen. It resumed on the way back and was accompanied by blows to John's head. Although Williams could not see where the whacks were coming from he could hear them pounding against his father and he witnessed red marks appearing on his face.

The punches were delivered with such intensity that at one point they rendered John stunned. Defeated, he sat down on a log by the road. "Then, his face commenced jerking with fearful contortions, soon his whole body. And then his shoes would fly off as fast as I could put them on," Williams' diary states.

Then the jubilant voice of the spirit filled the air. "I raised myself up to hear the reviling sound of derisive songs piercing the air with terrorizing force. As the demonic shrieks died away in triumphant rejoicing, the spell passed off, and I saw the tears chasing down Father's yet quivering cheeks. The trace of faltering courage marked every line of his face with a wearied expression of fading hope," Williams writes.

John confided to his son that he would not survive the persecution much longer ... that "it" was killing him through slow torture.

"My heart bleeds now at every pore as I pen these lines," Williams details. "Refreshing my memory with thoughts of the terror that possessed me then in anticipation of a fearful tragedy that might be enacted before Father could move from his position [on the side of the road]. That moment, my father turned his eyes upward and lifted his soul to Heaven in a burst of fervent passionate prayers such as I had never heard him utter before."

John Bell prayed that he and his family would be delivered from their "unknown devastating enemy." He then stood and returned to the house without further incident — but he never left it again.

(Section III of this book is devoted to the original Bell family stories, based on the diary of Williams Bell.)

Section I:

Living On The World's Most Haunted Property

Chris had no idea she was embarking upon an odyssey that would take her back two thousand years

Chapter One

Entrusted With The Land ... And Its Truth

The secret — the answer to the mystery behind the infamous Bell Witch haunting started to unravel and come to light soon after the Kirby family bought the historic property in 1993. But how much credence can be given to their claims? After all, who would buy such a farm?

Are they opportunists seeking to spin a fortune and capitalize on a sacred truth? Or are they just plain strange?

Neither. The Kirbys, it seems, were destined to be the caretakers of this most unusual land. They were chosen to unravel the mystery and to bring the truth to light through this book.

Indeed, every dynamic needed for the task, they possess. Yet, they are endearingly ordinary people caught up in the midst of something truly extraordinary.

Chris and Walter Kirby did not buy their one hundred acres of land and move there because it is the infamous Bell Witch Cave and Farm. They did so in spite of that fact.

"Our dream was to own a tobacco farm," explained Walter, a native Tennessean. "We saved for years, but every time we put a contract on one, something happened and the deal fell through. It was like something was blocking our every effort."

Meanwhile, forty miles away the Eden family (who owned and farmed the Bell Witch property at the time) attempted to sell repeatedly and the deal fell through every time.

"The Edens dropped the price down. It was a good deal: beautiful land with rich soil right on the river. So, I put a contract on it halfway thinking nothing would come of it," Walter said. "And the deal went through like clockwork. It was strange ... like it was meant to be ... like whatever forces were blocking our efforts to buy a farm, suddenly lifted."

Honey, We've Bought a Farm

"Walter came in and told me we finally got a contract accepted on a farm," Chris recalled. "Then he sat down and said there was something about the farm he had to tell me. I think he was afraid I was going to throw a fit and refuse to live on the Bell Witch Farm — and that our lifelong dream of owning a farm would be dashed or at least further delayed."

But Chris didn't balk at the news or even hesitate. In fact, she was expecting it.

"I had visited a psychic a few weeks earlier. She told me we were going to get a farm but to be prepared — there was something very peculiar about it. She said there was a highly supernatural energy there inside of a structure. She didn't know what type of structure it was only that it was apart from the house and it was permanent on the land," she said.

"I couldn't fathom what type of structure would be fixed to the land. But when Walter told me that the cave was part of the deal, I knew immediately we were buying the farm we were supposed to have. Besides, I had told Walter that whatever farm we bought I wanted a job on it. And since the Edens had opened the cave for public tours, this farm came ready-made with a job for me as a tour guide," Chris added.

In addition to her passion for psychic phenomena, Chris is a history and genealogy buff — a dedicated seeker of facts and truths. Long before they bought this historic landmark, her days were often spent doing family research at the Tennessee State Archives.

Chris' natural curiosity and thirst for truth proved to be the catalyst for unraveling a mystery that has captivated the world for centuries.

"After I learned that we were buying the Bell Witch Farm I was immediately excited about owning a piece of land with all of that history behind it — that even a U.S. president had visited," Chris said. "I thought about how intriguing it was going to be to research the Bell family who lived here two hundred years ago."

Chris had no idea that she was embarking upon an odyssey that would take her back more than two thousand years.

The Kirbys went to sign the papers, making the historic property their own. Afterward, Walter Kirby looked the seller in the eye and said, "Okay, the deal is done. You have nothing to gain and nothing to lose. I just want to know the truth. Is there something supernatural about this place?"

Eden looked him squarely in the eye and answered, "Son, you had better believe it."

"I knew it wasn't my imagination, because I called a friend and she could hear it over the phone"

Chapter Two

The Journey Begins With The Sounds of Horror

The Kirbys' journey to the truth begins with a surprising mentality: they didn't believe in the Bell Witch. "The truth is, if we had believed wholeheartedly in it we wouldn't have bought the place; but we didn't," Chris admitted. "And the fact that so many people do believe in it and therefore wouldn't consider living here helped to reduce the price. It allowed us to get more farm than we ever dreamed we could afford.

"We fell in love with it the minute we laid eyes on it. While we had always planned to own a farm, this one far exceeded our expectations. It's more beautiful than we ever dared to dream and we were tickled to death to own it from day one. The fact that it had a cave on it that's said to be haunted was just an interesting sidebar. We never imagined it would affect our day-to-day life.

"I think we're like most people when it comes to believing in such things. You can't fully believe it until you experience it yourself. But once you do witness it firsthand — when you actually experience it — nothing in this world can make you not believe in it. You know it for a fact," Chris added.

Some people who step foot on the Bell Witch property feel a presence, a supernatural energy, and the Kirbys were no

Inside The Bell Witch Cave

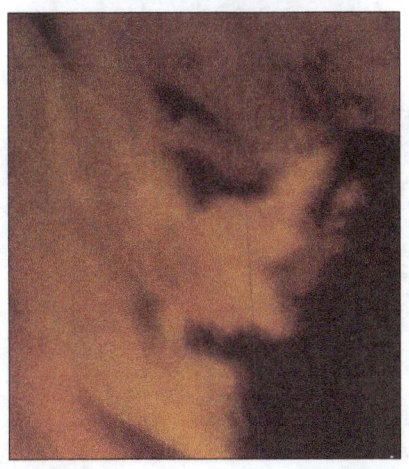
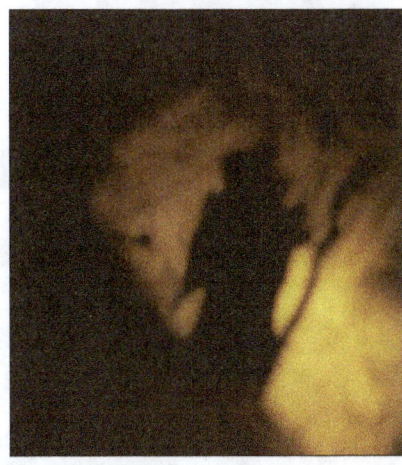

Historic Bell Witch Sites

The cabin that stands on the Bell Witch property today is an original Robertson County log cabin, built in the same era and style as the Bells' home.

The tombstone of John Bell.

The Bethel Meeting House is one of the churches believed to be frequented by the Bell Witch in the 1800s.

Drewry Bell's home in Adams, Tennessee.

exception. However, unlike others who define it as pure evil, the Kirbys felt benevolence — a spirit of welcome — confirming their belief that they were where they were supposed to be.

Moving in

On moving day, the modest brick house on the Bell Witch Farm, built by the Edens twenty-eight years earlier was teeming with hard work, confusion and anxiety over treasured pieces of furniture being nicked as they were hauled through the door: in essence, the typical nightmare that anyone who has ever moved experiences.

There was enough real "horror" going on that they didn't have the time or energy to worry about ghosts. Initially, only Chris and Walter's twelve-year-old daughter, Candy, moved to the farm with them. Their oldest daughter, Melinda, was nineteen and already out on her own. Their son, Brian, eighteen, was so close to high school graduation that he stayed in Nashville with his grandparents to avoid having to change schools during his senior year.

On the Kirbys' first night on the farm, after they had all collapsed with exhaustion into their beds, when all was quiet and dark and they had drifted into a deep sleep, they were startled awake by a crashing noise. It sounded like a large glass pitcher filled with water falling onto the wooden floor and shattering. All three members of the family sprang from their beds and sprinted for the light switches in their rooms.

"What on earth was that?" Chris called out to her daughter whose bedroom was across the hall.

"I don't know," Candy replied, as she stumbled sleepily out into the hallway.

Walter ambled out into the kitchen feeling his way around the unfamiliar room for the light switch. Finding it, he flipped it on but saw nothing amiss. Meanwhile, Chris checked the two bathrooms and found nothing. The pair met up in the

living room with Candy trailing behind.
"We didn't see anything that could have made that racket. Everything was still stacked in moving boxes so we convinced ourselves that a box had shifted, something inside had broken and we would find it in the morning. We also considered the possibility that a squirrel had gotten into the basement and knocked something over. Everything looked okay and we were exhausted so we went back to bed; however, this time we left some lights on," Chris recalled.

Echoes of the Bell Witch

The next morning, Chris spotted a small book lying on the kitchen counter that the Eden family had left for them as a housewarming gift. Entitled *Echoes of the Bell Witch in the Twentieth Century*, the journal chronicles the experiences of the Eden family on the farm.

"I took it out on the side porch with my coffee, sat down on the steps and started thumbing through it," Chris said.

The book fell open in her hands to page thirty, entitled "Breaking Glass." The chapter details a common occurrence in the Eden home that is described as a crashing noise in the night. "... as if someone had dropped a glass water pitcher on the floor."

Chris' hands went limp and the book fell to the ground. "I just thought, oh no, this can't be happening," she recalled. "I know that sounds funny coming from someone who just bought the Bell Witch Farm. But it was kind of like being in a bad car wreck. You know the possibility is there every time you get behind the wheel of your car, but it's still shocking and traumatic when it happens. You never really think it will happen to you. And to say that you hope it never does is an understatement."

She took the book back into the house, tucked it away in a kitchen drawer and said nothing to her family about it.

A Most Unsettling Settling in

Walter took great pride in finally owning his own farm. He immediately planted tobacco in the fields and started clearing away hundreds of years of brush. (Within weeks, several acres around the house had been transformed into park-like beauty.)

On their second day in the house, Walter was working outside and Candy was in her new school. Chris was organizing the kitchen and listening to the radio when she heard a loud rumble in the hallway that leads to the bedrooms. She turned the radio off and stood silently, listening. Then the racket erupted again. This time, she could identify it as sounding like someone walking around in the bedroom and opening drawers to the dresser.

"Walter, is that you?" she called out.

The noise stopped abruptly as if responding to her voice, but there was no answer.

"Is that you, Walter?" she repeated. Still no reply, but the noise started up again.

Chris didn't go into the hallway. Instead, she opened the side door and stepped outside to see if she could spot her husband in the yard or in the fields.

Not finding him, she walked completely around the house and was beginning to feel easier, believing that he must have been in the house or in the basement and he had made those sounds. However, when she got to the driveway, her knees weakened. His truck was not there — he was gone.

"I just wanted to get in my car and drive away," she said. "But my handbag was back in the bedroom and my keys were in it. I was not going back into that house to get them. Something or someone was in there. There was no question about that."

Too frightened to go back inside, she resigned herself to staying busy outdoors until Walter came home. When he did, she went back into the house and started cooking dinner.

Later that night, Chris finished washing the dishes and stepped into the living room where Walter was watching the news on television. Sheepishly, she began telling him about the noise in the bedroom and about the Edens' experience with the sound of breaking glass.

Walter's response surprised her. He said, "There is something here, I know that. But I also know that whatever it is blocked anyone else from buying this place. We're supposed to be here. And I feel okay about it. I know everything will be all right."

The next morning, Walter was returning to his job with a trucking company in Nashville and Chris would be alone in the house all day.

The Noise Grew Louder and Louder

Before Walter left for work, Chris planted her handbag beside the kitchen door, just in case.

"Around ten o'clock I heard a sound, kind of like someone working in the basement," Chris recalled. "It was soft, barely audible at first. I was trying to figure out what it was. I thought maybe the dog had gotten into the basement and was getting into things. But then it grew louder and louder — into a horrible banging that sounded like someone dropping heavy tools on the concrete floor. I couldn't believe my ears.

"I knew it wasn't my imagination, because I called a friend and she could hear it over the phone. I grabbed my bag and flew out the door. I jumped in the car and floored it, yet my heart was probably racing faster than the engine. I didn't go back until it was time for Candy to come home from school," she added.

A similar scenario played out the next day. In fact, it continued to happen from time to time, though the time of day varied, as well as the spectrum of the sounds. Sometimes, it was the sound of the crashing phantom water pitcher. At other times, it was scratching noises, banging in the basement, popping sounds, or the chilling toll of voices — carrying on conversations in a nonexistent upstairs room. Additionally, there were moments of haunting, persistent footsteps heard coming up from the basement to the house.

Inexplicable noises were also occurring at night in the presence of the entire family. Yet, they never seemed as intrusive or frightening behind the backdrop of a blaring television, telephone conversations, laughter, and all the rest of the chaos that comes with an active family. Even the noises that came in the still of the night seemed less threatening with Chris' family around her.

"It goes without saying, I was feeling extreme anxiety about living here," Chris said. "It seemed like, whatever it is, was trying to run us off. Yet, I was conflicted, because on another level, I knew that I was where I was meant to be."

The farm was all at one time, a dream come true and a living nightmare. Chris states now, in retrospect, that she has an understanding of the paradox she was experiencing. Before anything could be revealed to her — before "they" exposed the truth and themselves — she had to be a believer. She had to know the *darkness* to move toward the *light*. Although she didn't realize it at the time, she was just beginning her voyage toward truth.

"There was never a defining moment or revelation when we all openly conceded we had moved into a haunted house. I guess down deep we always knew," she said.

The fact that the Kirbys' daughter lived on the Bell Witch Farm was hardly a novelty at her new school. The children of Adams, Tennessee have grown up with the legend at their back door. While some of the local children thought it was "cool" to spend the night with Candy on the farm, most gave it little thought.

Chris, who was routinely alone in the house, was the primary person having to struggle with the haunting.

"Eventually, I had a moment of truth when I vowed that whatever force was there was not going to run me out of my own home," she said.

Now, when she hears a sound, she follows it and checks it out. If she doesn't see anything, she resumes what she was doing.

"I just tell myself, there's no water pitcher crashing to the floor; there's no one dropping tools in the basement. They are false, deceptive sounds — which is a part of this haunting. And the only harm that sounds can bring is fright. And I can control my own fear," she said.

Digging Her Feet Into the Soil

Chris' steely resolve may be difficult for some to understand. Faced with her predicament, most people would likely have decided they had made a mistake in buying the farm, put it on the market and moved — even if it meant taking a financial dive. Yet, Chris' tenacity is one of the major components that makes her a perfect owner of the Bell Witch Farm. Something inside of her made her accept her situation — and dig her heels into that farm.

To understand what "home" means to Chris, one would have to know a little about her past. She is the granddaughter of German immigrants who came to the United States, settling in Kentucky in search of the "American Dream." But the generations before her never found it. Although her parents raised her in a loving home with Christian values, they lived in financial destitution and never owned a home. Chris was determined that she would have the American Dream.

She and Walter met shortly after she graduated from high school. He was in the Army, stationed at nearby Fort Knox. When they married, they moved into a small, two-bedroom, shingled cottage owned by his parents, which sat just feet from his parents' back door in a suburb of Nashville. Although it was decent housing and eventually deeded over to them, they never felt a sense of privacy or homeownership. Nevertheless, they lived there for twenty years, saving money for their farm.

Then came the contract rejections. Farm after farm slipped through their fingers as if they were cursed. Then, finally, a "yes."

In a real sense, the Bell Witch Farm is the only home Chris has ever called her own. Come what may, she is not leaving it. That is not to say she is never afraid — she is — but she relies upon her inner strength. She leans on her faith in God to protect her and her family. She's also able to draw a distinction between the cave and her house. She knows the venom that spills over into the walls of her home and onto the fertile acres of farmland, emits from the cave. The cave is the source of the horror.

And she never, ever, goes in it alone ....

"You're not dealing with one entity, there are many spirits here"

Chapter Three

Eerie Photographs

Initial realization that the Kirbys are not alone on their farm went beyond the sounds of horror — as dozens of spirits began to reveal themselves in photographs.

Shortly after moving in, Chris set out on a walk across the land with her camera, photographing the waterfall that cascades from the bluff into the river and the magnificent centuries-old oak trees that grace the land. However, there were no photos of the cave to be taken; she'd walked down to the mouth of it but instinct had stopped her from entering.

When her film was developed, the first twelve photos appeared normal ... but the thirteenth photo on the roll took her breath away.

This photo, taken above a sinkhole (where a portion of the cave had collapsed hundreds of years ago) is eerily saturated with white ghostly images, each seeming to convey a message to her: We are here and we will not be ignored.

"You can talk yourself into denial or anything else when you are just hearing noises. They come and go," Chris said. "But a photo is something you can hold in your hand. It's tangible — and seeing is believing. What I couldn't understand was if the land is haunted by the so-called Bell Witch, why are there so many images in the photograph? What is going on here?"

Not knowing where else to turn, Chris contacted the psychic she had consulted before buying the farm and invited her for a visit.

The psychic walked the land with Chris and they entered the cave together, treading into its damp realm of darkness. The cave itself is physically amazing, comprised of two large chambers (or rooms). A long narrow hallway leads from the entrance to the first room, then another trails from the first room to the back room.

The Empty Tomb

In the first chamber, embedded in stone, is the small tomb of a Native American girl whom anthropologists determined died from a gunshot wound to the chest in the 1700s or early 1800s. Today, the tomb lies forebodingly open and empty — its remains absconded by vandals decades ago.

In the back room, a gigantic rust-colored flowstone protrudes from the wall which has been estimated by archaeologists to be an astounding eight million years old. Small tunnels (mere crawl spaces) lead from the back of the cave and extend approximately ten miles beneath rural Robertson County.

Like the rest of the cave, these channels were created naturally over countless centuries as water flows from an underground spring into the Red River.

On top of the first room, above the natural rock ceiling, is a second layer (or story) of tunnels.

Most interesting to history buffs is that on the wall of the first room is a ledge, scorched black from torches that illuminated the cave centuries ago.

"You're not dealing with one entity," the psychic told Chris. "There are many spirits here." She described one in particular as a small boy in overalls, about five years old. "He's afraid to cross over into the spirit world," she explained.

"But why is he here? Why are any of them here? Did they used to live here? Did they die here?" Chris asked.

"No," the psychic replied. "The cave is most likely a portal — a point at which spirits cross over from this world to the next. Many souls may linger here for a short time, or conceivably for an indefinite time, not wanting to go to the other side. They would most likely be people who weren't prepared to die — who went suddenly, or even violently. Souls who accept that their life here is over would logically pass through and cross over without incident. It's those who are angrily hanging on that act out so violently. Or, in the case of the little boy, are simply frightened and mischievous."

Though intrigued by the psychic's theory, Chris found it hard to comprehend ... until the image of a little boy in overalls showed up in a photo taken near the cave, as have the likenesses of other spirits — some as glowing white lights or orbs and others, like the boy, in ghostly human form. Most of these photos have been taken by people on tours of the cave, with duplicates sent to the Kirbys.

Another photo, taken of two girls sitting on a rock just outside the cave, shows a two-headed snake slithering up the leg of one of the girls. The snake was not visible when the photo was taken.

The Boy Who Disappeared

One rather disturbing photo was taken of a school group on a field trip at the farm. The teens are all smiles, sitting in two rows, one in front of the other. Several had their arms draped around the neck of a friend sitting next to them. But one of the teens who was seated on the front row is completely transparent in the photo. His friend is left with his arm draped around air and the legs of the person behind the vanished teen show through as if nothing was there at all.

"The teacher who sent me this photo was upset about the boy disappearing from it. She was afraid that it was a bad omen. But the kid who disappeared and all of his friends think it's cool," Chris said.

While the strange photos convinced the Kirbys that the psychic was probably correct in her assessment that there is far more than one paranormal energy inhabiting their farm, especially the cave — that, in fact, there's an ongoing flow of spirits — Chris and Walter were left with many unanswered questions. How did this phenomenon come into being? Why here? How can any of it ever be truly substantiated?

They never dreamed the mystery would soon unravel.

(All photos described in this book are on display at the Historic Bell Witch Cave.)

They felt a chill pass over and through them

Chapter Four

Throwing Open The Gates Of Hell

Though Chris had come to terms with the phenomenon occurring inside her home (as well as anyone could), her biggest hurdle was still to come as opening day for the cave tours neared.

The former owners of the cave had kept it closed during the winter because of the high volume of water that flows through it during those months and the Kirbys held to that schedule, opening on the first weekend in May with the final day of the season being October 31.

"The Edens installed an iron gate at the entrance to the cave to keep intruders out and there were electric lights strung up inside the cave, but we still had to do some work before we opened it," Chris said. "We had to rake out the rocks that the flowing water had left behind on the floors during the winter so that the rest of the water could flow out of the hallways. There's always a little water on the floor that trickles from the spring, but it dams up knee-deep during the winter months."

The morning before the cave was scheduled to open, Chris and her daughter, Candy, ventured toward it with heavy rakes in tow. When the mouth of the cave came into sight, they paused for a moment to muster their courage. They had a long day of work ahead of them. People would be coming the next day to go in the cave and it was their job, their responsibility, to make it safe for them.

They were determined to stay focused on the job at hand. If she was going to give tours, Chris knew she had to get a grip on her fear of the cave.

She put the key in the lock of the gate and turned it. Though her heart was pounding heavily and her hands trembling, she tried to conceal her fear from Candy. With Walter at work, if Candy backed out of helping her, the job would not get done. Chris was not going in alone.

The level of energy at the mouth of the cave is, at times, immense. As Chris reached for the gate and swung it open, she experienced a sinking feeling, as if she were throwing open the gates of Hell. Slowly they walked inside, found the light switch and flipped it on.

They Were Not Alone in the Cave

Before she had time to think about anything, Chris set her rake down on the floor in the first hallway and began raking the rocks while Candy ventured on to the first room. The rhythmic sound of rock raking quickly grew familiar. First comes the clang of the rake making contact with the rock floor, then the scraping noise as the tool bumps across it, and finally, the sound of the small rocks hitting together. Next, there is a pause as the rake is drawn back and the sounds are repeated.

They worked steadily with Candy raking the rocks from the first room out into the front hallway and with Chris taking them from that point, out the mouth of the cave. (Though starting at the back of the cave might have seemed more strategically sound, in their eyes, inching their way toward the back was a lot safer.)

After a couple of hours of continual work, Chris called out that she was taking a short break. Having cleared the first room of rocks, Candy picked up her rake and entered the second hallway, going deeper into the cave. All was quiet, but before Candy could draw back her rake, she suddenly heard the sound of raking coming from the *back* of the cave.

Knowing that her mother could not (and would not) have possibly squeezed passed her in the narrow hallway to get to the back room without her knowledge, Candy stood perplexed, frozen and listening. It sounded like raking, but there was no pause in it, just the constant sound of a rake scraping against the floor and the rocks hitting together. It was loud and it was coming closer and closer toward her.

Instinctively, she drew the rake up off the floor with both hands, positioning its steel teeth in front of her like a shield. Then she started running toward the entrance of the cave. When she met up with her mother in the first hallway, she grabbed onto her, screaming, "Get out of here!"

Chris looked into Candy's face, witnessing a terror that she had never seen on her daughter before. She was deathly white, trembling all over.

"What's wrong? What happened?" Chris shouted as she clasped onto her daughter, trying to hold her still.

"There is someone else in there raking rocks! Just listen!" Candy screamed.

Chris hadn't heard anything out of the ordinary. She had assumed that her daughter was creating any raking noise emitting from the back of the cave. She immediately tried to dispel Candy's fears to keep her from abandoning the job.

"Oh, Candy. The gate was locked and the lights were out when we came in. There's no way anyone could be in here," she said. "Besides, if there was someone in here, they wouldn't be raking rocks for us. It must have been some kind of echo."

"Just listen!" Candy screamed.

Chris listened, suddenly hearing a huge commotion, which by now was coming from the first room. It sounded like hundreds of rocks hitting together and the noise was moving toward them. Chris threw down her rake and they both fled the cave at breakneck speed. They retreated up the hill, not slowing down until they had reached the relative safety of their home.

Later in the day, Chris came to terms with the fact that they had to go back in the cave and finish the job.

"I kept thinking that maybe somewhere in the cave, a pile of rocks had dammed up and we had created a little landslide," she said. "But there was no use trying to convince Candy of that. The truth is, I couldn't even convince myself of it. After all of the strange sounds we had heard in the house, we both knew that the noise in the cave was being made by something supernatural."

Candy refused to go back at first but Chris used the same reasoning on her daughter that she has learned to use so effectively on herself: nothing had hurt them. It was just a noise and noises don't hurt you. Though this time, they would take their large, black dog, Partner, with them.

'It Was As Real To Us As We Were To Each Other'

Nothing seemed amiss when they reentered the cave. There had been no landslide of rocks. Chris and Candy picked up their rakes and began working again, this time, side by side, keeping each other in sight. Everything went fine until they approached the crook in the second hallway.

Partner was up ahead of them, around the corner and out of sight, when they heard him growl. They stopped raking, stood still and listened as his growl grew louder and more ferocious.

"I'll bet some kind of animal has gotten in here," Chris whispered as she and Candy held on to each other and slowly, with minced steps, continued down to the turn in the hallway where they saw Partner crouched in attack position. The hairs on his back were bristled up. His mouth was snarled, exposing his teeth.

He began barking and snapping, actually biting, but there was nothing there — nothing that could be seen.

They both felt a chill pass over and through them that cut

to the bone, filling them with dread. They stood frozen in fear, clutching on to each other. Then, just as suddenly, there was warmth again. Partner instantly calmed down, wedged himself between Chris' feet and whimpered.

"Whatever was in there passed on through," Chris said. "We couldn't see it, but we could feel it — it was as real to us as we were to each other."

Images Appear In Photos

The thirteenth photo on a roll of film that Chris Kirby took on the farm is eerily sated with ghostly images. It was taken above a sinkhole where a portion of the cave collapsed hundreds of years ago.

The cave's entrance is a common site for some very uncommon occurrences. Above: the Kirbys' daughter, Candy, sits on a rock in front of the cave. The burly man who showed up in the photo with her is not of this world.

Candy Kirby is seated in front of the cave with a friend behind her. Though her friend is real (and perfectly normal), notice that the arm draped around Candy's neck is too long and looks more like a leg and foot than an arm and a hand.

Ghostly images show up in this photo at the cave's entrance.

"Oh, my gosh, I can't believe what we just saw"

Chapter Five

First Sightings

Opening day at the cave came with much trepidation. "I was so afraid. But I just had to keep telling myself that people were going to pay me to guide them through the cave and I had to buck up, be in charge and make myself go through with it — no matter what," Chris said. "At least I wouldn't be alone. The larger the group, the better."

The first group to gather was comprised of four couples, including a woman who said she was a psychic. That gave Chris some reassurance. "Psychics have a profound understanding of the supernatural and are generally comforting in fearful situations," she said.

She led the group down to the cave and put the key in the lock, hoping that they didn't notice her hands trembling. She wondered if they sensed that she was just as frightened as they were — probably more.

As they entered the passageway to the first room, Chris began giving the tour talk that she had developed from her studies on the Bell Witch. But when they entered the first room, the psychic interrupted her, relaying the same information that the first psychic had given weeks earlier — that she could feel the presence of many, many spirits — not just one.

Chris led the group onward, descending down the second hallway, which is only wide enough for single-file passage, when they all began to hear a deep raspy sound ascending from the back room. It was soft at first and Chris tried to ignore it, focusing on her talk. But the sound grew louder, taking on the distinct sound of a human or an animal gasping for air. In the same moment, that eerily familiar chill filled the air. Chris went silent, came to a dead halt and started backing up in the narrow hallway.

But the psychic was right up behind her, nudging her forward, saying, "Go ahead. They won't hurt you."

Chris stepped to the side, thinking, "Are you crazy? *You* go ahead."

The psychic took the lead and the others followed, with Chris falling into the middle of the group, going along with the flow ... each step drawing the vexatious breathing sound closer and closer, as if it was luring them into the back room.

As the group approached the entrance to the back room, the breathing sound stopped — and so did the people. Chris was behind them and couldn't see into the room, but they weren't going in. They were bottled up, frozen at the entrance of it, mesmerized, all looking up toward the ceiling.

No one uttered a sound. No one dared to breathe. But as if on cue, they all turned in the same instant and bolted back down the hallway toward the entrance of the cave, shoving Chris forward with the psychic behind her, now pushing her to move faster in the other direction.

They flew out of the cave, taking the steep hill up to the house in a flash, screaming, "Oh, my gosh! Did you see that? Did you see that thing? Oh, my gosh! I can't believe what we just saw!"

By the time they reached the top of the hill, all nine adults were bent over at the waist, trying to catch their breath.

The people were hysterical. Like a number of others over the decades (including the years that the Edens gave tours) the tourists described seeing a large mass of white, smoky haze moving across the ceiling. Some of the people in the group described it as looking like the image of a young woman in a long, flowing gown. Others described it simply as a thick mist that appeared to be taking the form of "something."

The cave visitors were ecstatic. They had gotten more than their money's worth. They had a story to tell the rest of their lives.

Chris, on the other hand, had another group of people waiting to be taken inside the cave. Although she had seen nothing, she had heard plenty and understandably had profuse reservations about reentering the cave.

She needed help and she needed more help than her dog could provide. She began looking out over the fields for her six-foot-one, 250-pound husband. Fortunately, it was Saturday and he was home. She spotted him, already walking toward her. He had been on his tractor when he witnessed the group — nine adults — bolting hysterically up the hill from the cave. It wasn't the image he had expected to see from Chris' first tour and rightfully assumed that her maiden voyage had been baptized by fire.

Chris began marching toward him, focused on speaking with him out of earshot of her customers. With every step, her fear was transforming into anger, which in the moment, was directed at him.

"What a deal," she was thinking. "He's out here in the sunshine, doing his farm work, while I'm giving tours through Hell."

When they got within a few yards of each other, Walter called out, "What's going on?"

"You're going with me on the next tour. That's what's going on," she snapped. "Come on. Right now. People are waiting." She turned and marched back toward the group with Walter still puzzled, but complying.

On the next tour, Walter led the group in, while Chris brought up the rear, giving the talk.

"If Walter had known the talk, I wouldn't have gone back in at all," she said. "But he didn't, so I had no choice. And I guess it was just as well. I had to get right back in the saddle of the horse that threw me."

That next tour was uneventful. In fact, months passed before anyone claimed to have seen it again, though less dramatic apparitions are common inside the cave.

"Sometimes, we'll see a hazy ripple in the air along the floor that looks like a heatwave on a hot road, which makes no sense, since it's always about 60 degrees in there," Chris said.

"At other times, we'll see something that looks like a puff of smoke or a cloud floating through the room or down a hall. Glowing balls of light also appear pretty frequently in photos taken inside the cave."

After her first horrifying day as a Bell Witch Cave tour guide, Chris was lying in bed awake half the night trying to bolster her own courage for the next day by affirming: Things that I hear don't hurt me and things I see don't hurt me.

But she wondered, is there anything in the cave that can hurt me or my customers? She got out of bed, went into the kitchen and pulled the Edens' book out of the drawer. It was time to read about their experiences on the farm. She had to know.

Worst Fears Confirmed

The Edens' book relays many of the same experiences that the Kirbys have endured, from the sounds of an occasional scream to sightings of dark shadows creeping through the cave. When Eden was taking one group through the cave and they witnessed the ghostly image, a young woman fainted and had to be carried out of the cave and revived with cold water from the spring.

The book also confirmed Chris' worst fears. The manifestations go beyond sights and sounds to physical encounters, such as:

- An unseen force physically grabbed Eden on several occasions inside the cave.

- A girl on a tour was slapped so hard in the face by an invisible force that it knocked her to the ground, and red fingerprints were still visible on her jaw after the group had exited the cave.

- The Edens' book also details a tour of the cave taken by five soldiers from nearby Fort Campbell. When the group reached the back room, they sat down and began talking with Eden about his experiences with the Bell Witch.
  One young soldier who was sitting on a ledge began scoffing at the myth, saying that he didn't believe in such things. Suddenly, that same soldier began to scream that something was squeezing him so tight that he couldn't breathe or move. Eden and the other soldiers thought he was joking at first. But when his pleas for help intensified, they looked at him, realizing that he was ghostly white and dripping wet as if someone had thrown a bucket of water on him.
  Eden reached out to pull the young soldier from his position on the ledge. His skin was wet and clammy and Eden couldn't budge him. Then the other four began pulling until they were finally able to free him from the force that bound him. He too was bathed off with cool spring water and carried out of the cave.

Chris put the book aside and stayed up the remainder of the night, drawing up a waiver of responsibility for people to sign before they enter the cave. It is not a gimmick.

"We've installed handrails on the path that lead to the cave. We have installed additional lights going to the cave and in the cave. We've made everything as safe as we possibly can. But we only own the physical structure," she said. "Beyond that, we have no control. And we can't risk a lawsuit. We're not willing to risk losing the farm and everything that we've worked so hard for due to something that's totally beyond our control."

Section II:

The Secrets Come To Light

"I couldn't think of a good reason why anyone would have human bones in a smokehouse"

Chapter Six

Discovery: Human Bones

Though the Kirbys felt that both of the psychics were correct in their assessments — that the cave contains a portal or a doorway into the spirit world and that many spirits inhabit their property at any given time — they never dreamed it would soon be proven.

A weather-beaten old smokehouse that stood forlornly on the farm concealed the first piece of the puzzle.

It was Chris who would feel inexplicably drawn to the smokehouse several weeks after the move.

"I walked down there, lifted the latch and opened the door," she recalled. "I thought the worst thing that I might encounter would be a snake or a spider."

She was wrong. Its contents were much, much worse. It contained human bones — leg bones, arms and part of a skull.

"My heart just stopped. I was speechless," she recalled. "The Edens seemed like nice normal people. But I couldn't think of a good reason why anyone would have human bones in a smokehouse."

Her mind ran the gamut of possible explanations — all horror stories yet each one led back to the same questions: Why would they leave them here for us to find? Why wouldn't they have buried them? Could there be a less sinister explanation?

It is true that remnants of death permeate the Bell Witch

Farm. Chris was learning from studying its history that there are dozens of graves on the property.

The Edens had informed her about a Native American graveyard on the land, comprised of about thirty graves. The age of those graves had been determined by a Nashville anthropologist to be two to three thousand years old. There are also Indian mounds down near the river.

Grave Robbery

Members of the Bell family are buried nearby, actually one farm over. As was customary in the South in those days, family cemeteries were established on the grounds of the homestead. But the Bell cemetery was approximately 300 yards from the house, and when the original farm was subdivided and split among the heirs, the cemetery was not on the same tract with the house and cave — which is the tract that the Kirbys now own.

The slaves of the Bell family are also buried in that same cemetery, marked with simple flagstones. Large indentions in the ground indicate that some of these graves have caved in, while others seem to have been completely robbed of their coffins and corpses.

There is also the missing skeleton of the Native American girl, abducted from her tomb inside the cave.

But the skeletal remains in the smokehouse were adult-size, clearly belonging to more than one person.

Chris summoned the county sheriff's office.

"There are a lot of Native American graves in this county and it's pretty common for them to get disinterred during farming, which is probably what happened here," the Robertson County Sheriff's Deputy said casually as he examined the bones. "But we'll send a sample to the state anthropologist, just to be sure. He can determine their age."

It was soon confirmed that the bones were human.

Their age was estimated to be two thousand years old and it's believed they belonged to members of the ancient Mississippi Mound Builders tribe. The Mound Builders inhabited the area for thousands of years but mysteriously vanished from the earth more than two thousand years ago. They buried their dead upright in their graves, in fetal positions, with their heads toward the sky, without the use of tombs or any other type of covering.

This explains accounts of the Bell family having unearthed a human jawbone during plowing, as well as why now, hundreds of years later, lower human extremities are beginning to surface. Significantly, according to the old Bell Witch books, the paranormal activities on the farm did not surface until the jawbone did.

The Bones Were Pointing the Way ...

While decimated Native American gravesites have always been notorious for manifesting hauntings, the Kirbys were about to discover that this is just one piece of the much larger Bell Witch puzzle.

"There are a lot of haunted places in America that were created by disturbed Native American graves," Chris said. "But that does not explain the spirits that are showing up in the photographs taken here. Those spirits appear to be Caucasians who, judging by their clothes, lived on this earth in relatively modern times, such as the frightened five-year-old boy in overalls. What possible connection could there be between the spirit of that little boy and Native Americans who were buried here two thousand years ago? Could there indeed be a portal inside the cave?

"We discovered that the disturbed Native American graves on the property are not the whole answer to the haunting, but they were pointing us in the right direction," she added.

Regardless of the age of the bones, out of respect for

the dead, Chris wanted to return the skeletal remains to the ground.

With a shovel in hand, she walked to the spot that the Edens said embraced the Indian gravesite ... and found herself standing directly on top of the cave.

Even more chilling: the door may swing both ways, permitting the dead to visit the world of the living

Chapter Seven

Captured On Video

Soon after moving to the farm, the Kirbys began receiving frequent requests from paranormal investigators who wanted to set up twenty-first century high tech equipment inside the cave for investigative purposes.

Wanting to unravel the mystery themselves, they consented to allow a team to go in, headed by renowned paranormal investigator Bob Schott.

Schott is known for his use of the most advanced types of equipment and the latest techniques available.

The investigative team arrived armed with state-of-the-art temperature monitors, night vision equipment, electromagnetic field fluctuation detectors and a computerized system to detect any type of change in a range of energy fields, called MESA (Multi Energy Sensory Array).

Immediately inside the cave, MESA began to spike, while the thermometers showed sudden drops in temperature. Although the gages generally recorded the temperatures in the lower sixties, on two different occasions, temperatures plummeted suddenly to fifty-two degrees as "something" was felt passing the crew, only to rise again after it had cleared the area. This confirmed the many similar experiences that the Kirbys have encountered in the cave when sudden chills are evident while the presence of something unseen is felt passing through. It is usually during these times that Chris' flashlight goes dark, the video cameras carried by tourists suddenly stop, and the dog begins to growl and back away from the area.

When Schott's team developed a photograph taken inside the cave at the exact moment of one of these drops in temperature, it revealed a glowing orb of light near the ceiling. Yet the most dramatic evidence was still to come.

At the Kirbys' urging, a video camera was set up overnight in the cave, trained on the deep, dark hole in the crook of the second corridor, leading to the back room. "If anything strange is going to happen, that's often where it happens," Chris said.

The low-light sensitive video camera that Schott set up had been fitted with a Generation III Night Vision lens with a special infrared filter which is reportedly five times more sensitive than those used by the U.S. military. It captures 50 images per second.

The results were shocking.

On the film, captured in a few seconds, a type of doorway suddenly appears on the screen and slides open, just long enough to allow the passage of two human-like forms as they transcend from left to right — from the physical world into the spirit world. When the doorway slides shut behind them, it all vanishes from the screen.

Schott had captured on film what the psychics knew intuitively: Inside the Bell Witch Cave is a portal — a rip in the veil that separates the world of the living from the world of the dead.

Expert Opinions

Being an investigator, Schott sought analysis of his findings from a number of experts. He submitted the tape to two major independent corporations that specialize in infrared and electro-optics and provide advanced defense technology to the U.S. military. They were both admittedly stumped by what they observed on the film from the Bell Witch Cave. They issued the following statements:

> "I have no explanation for the vortex or doorway depicted in the film. It is truly an unexplainable phenomenon."
> **— B.E. Myers of Electro Optics**

> "With regard to the translucent sliding doorway effect, I have no explanation for this phenomenon."
> **— Alan Harding of Litton Electro-Optics**

Schott then turned to leaders in the field of paranormal phenomena. Author and renowned expert in the field of paranormal activity, Rosemary Ellen Guiley, agreed with Schott that the doorway was indeed a portal between worlds and that there are likely scores of spirits in and around the cave at all times.

"We were absolutely stunned to see tangible proof that there's a portal between worlds inside the cave," Walter said. "While we had assumed the psychics were correct in their theories, we never dreamed in a million years that we would be able to prove it — that we would have a picture of it!"

In those few haunting seconds captured on film, a mystery was solved that has perplexed the world since the Bells moved to the property more than two hundred years ago.

There are dozens, conceivably even hundreds, of spirits in and around the cave at any time as they pass through to the spirit world. It's no wonder that the Bell Witch Cave has earned notoriety as the most haunted spot in America.

Even more chilling, as Guiley noted, this doorway conceivably swings both ways, permitting the dead to visit the world of the living.

That could well explain why Native Americans considered this beautiful land cursed and abandoned it hundreds of years before the White man cast his lot upon it. It also explains what the Bell family had unknowingly walked into all those years ago.

But the photo of the portal did not solve the entire mystery. Questions still remained:

- How did the portal come into being? Is it a natural occurrence designed by the Creator of all things?

- Why is it in a rural Tennessee county of all places? Why not Bethlehem or some other established Holy Land?

- What connection is there, if any, between the Native American graves directly above the cave and the portal inside of it?

Bob Schott and Rosemary Guiley both speculated on the burial mound's proximity to the portal. They assumed that the ancient tribes knew about the portal and that they had buried their dead directly above it — so their relatives would not have far to travel to the spirit world.

That assumption was incorrect.

It sounds like magic, but the consequences are very, very real

Chapter Eight

The Final Piece Of The Puzzle

Once the Kirbys knew the truth — that the supernatural presence there is so much more than "a witch," they felt an obligation to share it with the world.

"We don't own the legend, nor the miracle that's been discovered here," Chris said. "We simply view ourselves as temporary caretakers of this most remarkable property. And for whatever reason, we have now been entrusted with its truth."

But they wanted to be careful about publishing a book. The story, they insisted, must be historically accurate and factual, devoid of commercial hype. This is a sacred site. Its honor and integrity must be preserved — its story must be presented with sensitivity.

The author of this book has been good friends with Chris and Walter for more than thirty years — since we were teenagers. They felt comfortable putting their trust in me. I am also a veteran investigative newspaper reporter and editor, dedicated to reporting the unbiased truth. Like many other newspaper reporters, my dream was to one day author a book of historic significance — to leave something behind that will live beyond my time on Earth. Ironically, I'm also the one who told the Kirbys about the Bell Witch. They had never heard of it, but I cut my teeth on the legend.

I couldn't have been more than five years old when I started visiting the library in the little village where I grew up. It was the town of Old Hickory, Tennessee, named for President Andrew Jackson, whose plantation is nearby. (Jackson was described as being as tough as an old Hickory tree — hence his nickname: Old Hickory.) I loved to hear the tales about the Bell Witch that old Mrs. Latimer, the librarian, used to tell. She was born on the Bell Witch farm around 1900 and grew up there, personally experiencing her hair being pulled and her cheeks slapped by an unseen force. Mrs. Latimer also, incidentally, passed along her love of books to me.

So thirty years later, when I began writing a book to reveal the secret behind the Bell Witch phenomenon, the pieces of my life seemed to slide into place. If the Kirbys were destined to live out their lives on the Bell Witch Farm, I was surely destined to record it in a book.

But while all of the pieces of my life had come together, pieces of the Bell Witch puzzle were still missing. How did that portal come into being? What was its relationship to the burial ground above it?

I immediately put my instincts and skills to work that have served me well as a reporter. Since the Mound Builders buried their dead above the cave, the cave was very sacred ground — a hallowed shrine. They would not have lived in it. But why are there scorch marks from torches inside of it? Did they perform ceremonies in there? What kind of ceremonies? What was going on in there thousands of years ago?

I went to the cave for the answer. My purpose was not to study the physical structure, but frankly, to seek guidance. This "thing," this phenomenon, was attempting to communicate — to be understood. Why else are entities repeatedly showing up in photographs and in form? Why else was the thing itself, the portal, revealed on film?

I walked into the first room of the cave alone and sat down

on a large rock next to the empty tomb. I closed my eyes, drawing in deep breaths as I waited, wistfully hoping against hope for some type of direction to be revealed to me.

Suddenly, I felt a surge of heat against my face and I opened my eyes. There before me were flames from a brilliant fire illuminating the ledge of the wall opposite me.

Stunned, I blinked in disbelief, thinking that when I opened my eyes again, the flames would be gone — but the fire continued to blaze. It wasn't dream-like; there was nothing vague about it. It was as real as any fire that I have ever seen or felt. I wanted to run but was unable to move. Then, in an instant, the flames were gone. The only thing left on the wall along the ledges were those blackened torch marks — not made minutes ago — but millenniums ago.

I walked over to the ledge and placed my hand against the wall where the flames had been just moments before. It felt as cool to the touch as any other part of the cave. What was being communicated to me? What did I need to learn about the torches that illuminated the cave thousands of years ago?

As soon as I got home, I turned to the Internet to learn everything that I could about the Mound Builders, whose torches once lighted the Bell Witch Cave. This led me to several books on the subject of the shamans, who were the spiritual leaders of the Mound Builders. It also led me to the final piece of the Bell Witch puzzle.

Yes, of course, the shamans performed spiritual rituals with torches. But what was the reason for the rituals?

The secret purpose of the Mound Builders' rituals, performed by the shamans, I learned, was to open a passageway between the world of the living and the world of the dead.[1]

---

[1] *Encyclopedia of Native American Shamanism: Sacred Ceremonies of North America* by W. Lyon

I could not believe what I was reading. I had to sort it all out in my mind to fully comprehend it:

- There is a portal in the cave.

- Ceremonies were performed in the cave.

- The purpose of the ceremonies was to open a portal.

If there was a doubt in anyone's mind that the image seen on Schott's film was a portal — this information squelched it.

More importantly, this information answered my final question about the link between the portal and the Indian mound above it.

The Mound Builders had not buried their dead on top of the cave so they would be near a portal. They had opened the portal in the cave because it was near the burial place of their dead.

It sounds like magic. But the consequences are very, very real.

The spirit quoted the Bible, sang hymns, and threw blasphemous tirades

Chapter Nine

New Light On Old Stories

With the knowledge we have today about the secret of the Bell Witch Cave, it's interesting to look back over the old Bell Witch books, viewing the historic accounts from a new perspective.

We submit that this new information does not debunk the old stories, but substantiates them instead. Moreover, the old stories, in turn, substantiate the new information.

As far as we have been able to determine, the two oldest and most reliable Bell Witch books are those written by members of the Bell family. Both of them clearly point to the existence of more than one spirit plaguing the family. Yet the authors more or less attribute these instances to the "trickery" of one all-powerful spirit such as its ability to sing with four distinctly different voices — all together — in harmony. When these same four voices (who, incidentally, had four different names) argued and fought among themselves, it was simply "the witch entertaining the spectators." When the spirit identifies itself one day as a child who was buried in North Carolina and on another day, as the spirit of an immigrant — the witch is "obviously lying."

The authors of these books, it seems, were bent on perpetuating the single-entity "Bell Witch" myth against all facts and reasoning.

The oldest of the books is based on the diary of one of the Bell children, Williams Bell, which he wrote in 1846. It is filled with his own eyewitness accounts of the events that occurred in his home.

However, since his brothers and sisters requested the diary not be published until every immediate member of the Bell family had died, it was not published until 1894 when it was penned and published by M.V. Ingram, entitled *Authenticated History of the Bell Witch*.

It's interesting that although Williams refers to the entity as "the witch" and as "Kate," he had this to say about its gender: "He, she or it — whatever may have been the sex, has never been divined."

The other authoritative book mentioned is *The Bell Witch Of Tennessee,* written in 1934 by Charles Bailey Bell, a great-grandson of John Bell. This book, like most subsequent Bell Witch books, is largely based on the original accounts published in Ingram's book. However, Charles also interviewed others who were eyewitnesses to these events.

Following are some examples from *The Bell Witch of Tennessee* which clearly indicate the existence of more than one spirit on the Bell Witch Farm. Some of these excerpts also eerily substantiate the recent discovery of the portal and its direct relationship to the Mound Builders.

- "The first words the spirit ever uttered were: 'I am the spirit of a person who was buried in the woods nearby, and the grave has been disturbed, my bones disinterred and scattered.'" Page 99

- At another time, the spirit said, "I am the spirit of an early immigrant." Page 102

- And still another revelation, "I am the spirit of a child buried in North Carolina." Page 114

- "The spirit was frequently in two or more places at the same time." Pages 31, 33

- The spirit had different voices. This fact was ignored and unreported in this book, except for one instance when John Bell Jr. is quoted referring to "... the voice most often used by the spirit." Page 195

- Two female members of the Bell family reported seeing four different entities in a field at the same time which proceeded to vanish before their eyes. Three of the spirits appeared to be female, one male. Page 148

- The spirit recites a personal conversation alleged to have taken place between Napoleon and one of his soldiers dying on the battlefield. At other points in time, it (or they) claim to have firsthand experiences from ancient Africa, Egypt, England, the West Indies, virtually the world over. Page 197

- "The spirit speaks in every language." Pages 150, 180

- "The spirit was sometimes kind, and at other times, cruel." Page 111

- The spirit quoted the *Bible* and sang hymns, and it threw "blasphemous tirades." Page 180

- When Andrew Jackson visits the farm, John Bell entertains him with stories about the Indian mounds and relics near the river, and specifically relays stories about the Mound Builders who used to inhabit his land. Page 66

- The Bells' daughter, Betsy, who was a primary target of the haunting, mentions the Indian mounds that she frequented to dig up relics. Page 72

- The spirit says, "I am not happy. I do not deny my hope for a day of happiness passed hundreds of years ago. I believe my present plight is for all eternity." Pages 180, 181

- After living with the horrendous haunting for years and seeking help from detectives, spiritual advisors and "witch hunters" from around the world, John Bell Jr. summed up his opinion of the spirit with chilling accuracy as "... belonging to a world of demons, not a part of this world, nor its own ... a wandering thing between this world and some other." Page 197

From Ingram's book, Williams Bell gives the following account of an entire "witch family" that invaded their home, though he insists it was all a production created by a single entity.

The Witch Family

"The next development was the introduction of four characters with four unique names, purporting to be a witch family, each one acting a part, making every night absolutely hideous in their high carnivals, using the most offensive language and uttering vile threats," Williams writes.

"Up to this time, the strange visitor had spoken in the same soft delicate voice, except when impersonating some individual. Now there were four distinct voices.

"Blackdog was the head of the family and spoke in a harsh feminine tone. The voices of Mathematics and Cypocryphy were different, but both of a more delicate feminine tone. Jerusalem spoke like a boy," Williams writes.

"These exhibitions were opened like a drunken carousel and became perfect pandemonium, frightful to the extreme, from which there was no escape.

"Father would most gladly have abandoned our home and everything and fled with his family to some far away scene to have escaped this intolerable persecution, but there was no hope, no escape. The awful thing had sworn vengeance, and for what cause it never named, nor could anyone ever surmise," Williams continues.

"Nevertheless, when the question of moving was discussed, it declared it would follow 'Old Jack' to the remotest part of the earth, and Father believed it.

"These demonic councils were introduced by singing, followed by quarreling with each other, employing obscene language and blasphemous oaths, making noises like a lot of drunken men fighting.

"The carousels were ended only at the command of Blackdog, who sent the family away on different errands of deviltry — though one or two remained to keep up the usual disturbance in different rooms at the same time [in our home].

"At other times the unity appeared more civil and would treat our company to some delightful singing, a regular concert of rich feminine voices, modulated to the sweetest cadence and intonation, singing any hymn called for with solemnity and wonderful effect.

"The carousels did not continue long, much to the relief and gratification of our family and friends. And afterward, the four demons or unity never, apparently, met again.

"It was plain old Kate from that time on who assumed all characters, good or bad, sometimes very pious and then extremely wicked," Williams concludes.

*Countless people have been knocked to the
ground and held by an unseen force*

Chapter Ten

Yes, There Is A 'Bell Witch'

Having gone to great lengths to establish the fact that the Bell Witch Cave and Farm are inhabited by not just one entity but many, the reality that one dominant spirit has endured there for at least two hundred years cannot be denied. Although it's inaccurate to call it a "witch" and unfortunate that the Bell name became attached to it, there is a Bell Witch.

This declaration is based on the following observations:

- While John Bell Jr.'s words, "... the voice used most often by The Spirit" substantiated the existence of more than one spirit in the last chapter, they also substantiate the existence of one dominant spirit.

- The Bell family had an ongoing relationship with one spirit whose theme carried over from day to day, such as its determination to kill John Bell. This spirit was also consistent in the nicknames that it assigned to members of the Bell family, such as its reference to Lucy Bell as "Luce," John Bell as "Old Jack" and to a neighbor as "Old Sugar Mouth."

- Many of the very same anomalies that played out in the Bell home in the 1800s occurred in the Eden home during the 1900s and continue in the twenty-first century home of the Kirbys. Although other families besides these three have owned the property over the years, they did not open the cave for tours or write books about their lives on the farm. So anything that did or did not happen during those years is unknown to the public.

  This author, however, does have second-hand knowledge of many strange occurrences that happened during the years that (the librarian) Mrs. Latimer's family lived on the farm, which would have been around 1900.

The following are some examples of the common occurrences on the farm transcending three centuries:

A Slap in the Face

- Red finger marks left by an apparent slap to the face are recurring in the old Bell Witch books. These blows were levied against numerous visitors to the farm, as well as members of the Bell family, particularly young Betsy.

- The Edens' book also reports slaps to the face. Once when Eden was taking a group of teenagers through the cave, one girl started walking out ahead of him, declaring that she didn't believe in the Bell Witch. Then, suddenly, she stumbled backward screaming that something had hit her. Eden helped her to her feet and out of the cave into the sunlight. There, he and the rest of the group witnessed a distinct red handprint across the girl's face — exactly like the ones frequently described as appearing on Betsy's face.

Retribution

- Swift and certain retribution against nonbelievers (and even those who show disrespect) has also been a recurring theme on the farm for two hundred years.

- One of the men in Andrew Jackson's party, who claimed to be a "witch slayer," was physically attacked by an unseen force with Jackson and others hearing the blows being meted out against the fellow. Members of the Bell family continually cautioned people not to taunt the spirit.

- Countless people being knocked to the ground and held by an unseen force have been reported but only after showing disrespect.

- On a Saturday night in the 1950s, three mischievous teenagers from Nashville ventured into the old Bell family cemetery. Finding the tombstone of John Bell, they loaded it into their car and headed back to Nashville, undoubtedly reveling in the belief they had pulled a prank that would make them legends. And in fact, they had. The driver of the car never made it home. He was killed when his car suddenly veered violently out of control and crashed. The other two boys were severely injured, and one of them paralyzed. The only unscathed item found among the wreckage was the tombstone of John Bell.

    Obviously wanting to rid the family of a "curse," the deceased boy's sister drove the tombstone back to the town of Adams, and under the veil of darkness, left it along the side of a rural road ... where it vanished. (If someone picked it up, they may not have lived long enough to brag about it.)

- To this day, people regret committing the slightest infraction against this land. "A woman who was touring the cave recently asked if she could take a pebble from the creek bed inside the cave to have as a keepsake," Chris recalled. "I told her I didn't mind, but I also had to warn her. Others have done that and every one of them brought it back right away."

  The woman said that was nonsense, stuck a pebble into her pocket and left. An hour later she came back and thrust it into Chris' hand. She was crying. Blood was streaming down both of her legs and her arms were scraped. She said that a powerful force had knocked her to the ground.

Horrific Sounds and Other Anomalies

- Heavy, raspy breathing heard inside the cave is another recurring phenomenon that has transcended the centuries, as are the sounds of chains dragging and footsteps along the gravel floor of the cave (as well as down the hallway inside the house). Horses, buggies and, in more recent years, automobiles, stop and refuse to go one minute, then take off the next. The sound of the phantom water pitcher breaking and unexplained lights in the treetops persist, as do images of ghostly figures, some with one head, some with two and some with no head at all.

- Family cats hiss and arch their backs in response to unseen energies inside the cave and, ultimately, they steer clear of the cave altogether.

- Perhaps the most disturbing occurrences that played out in the Bell home and are now occurring in the Kirby home are audible voices, precisely impersonating the voices of people. (There are numerous instances of this reported in the diary of Williams Bell. One of them is given in the third section of this book.)

- "Several times I've been in the back room of the cave changing a light bulb and have heard Chris bringing a tour group in," Walter said. "I can hear her telling them all about the cave, and I hear the people asking questions and talking amongst themselves. Then when I walk out, there's no one around. Chris is still up at the parking lot."
  Chris and Candy have both experienced that same phenomenon. "The passage between the rooms of the cave is so narrow that people have to walk single-file through it. So, we only take one group in at a time," Chris said. "I don't want to be coming out with a group and have Candy coming in with one. But several times, I've been in the back room and have heard Candy entering the cave with another group. It always sounds so real, it fools me every time. I think, 'Now why is she coming in already?' But when I go out, she nor her phantom group are anywhere in sight."

Even more disturbing is when the voice being impersonated belongs to a loved one who has departed ....

*When 'it' mocks the voice of your
dead father ... it's personal*

Chapter Eleven

Living With 'It' Today

In the still of darkness one night, Walter Kirby awoke to the whispered tones of his father's voice — so close that he felt the warmth of his breath against his cheek.

He sat up, edged his feet to the floor and rubbed his eyes. Was it a dream? Was it a visit from beyond the grave? Or was it the cruel, demonic mimicking of his father's voice who had been laid in his grave just four days earlier?

Walter's heart was pounding. He sat motionless on the side of the bed, his feet transfixed to the floor. Then out of the darkness, the voice beckoned to him again — calling his name in a pitch that had risen beyond whispers.

The incident would not be mentioned at the breakfast table the next morning (and only through coaxing was it relayed for this book).

Hearing his late father's voice in the darkness was different than hearing the sound of a nonexistent glass water pitcher hitting the floor and shattering during the night. This was different than phantom footsteps heard lumbering down the hallway or seeing mysterious lights aglow in the treetops. Those occurrences play out regardless of who is in the house. But when "it" whispers in your ear — and mocks the voice of your dead father ... it's personal. It's terrifying, no matter who you are, no matter where you live.

"There are evil spirits here. There's just no denying that," Walter said. "But there are good spirits here, too. One evening

I was walking across the yard, heading into the house, when suddenly I heard the loudest crashing noise that I've ever heard in my life coming from the barn. I couldn't imagine what it was, because the only thing in the barn was a little calf.

"I flung open the barn door and saw that little calf lying there real still. I walked over to it and knelt down beside him. He was breathing, but I couldn't arouse him. So, I called the vet to come out. As it turned out, the calf was very sick and wouldn't have made it through the night without being put on an antibiotic. Whatever, or whoever, made that sound, did it to get my attention and save the calf's life," Walter said.

Keeping 'it' at Bay

"An old Native American came to the cave, performed an ancient ritual and hung a corn-rattler for us. He said it would keep the spirits calm and I think it has helped some," Chris said. "We don't mind hearing an occasional groan, or the sound of someone running through the cave or banging noises when we're giving a tour. That's good for business. People come back and they bring their friends.

"But when it knocks someone to the ground and holds them down, and they get up screaming and run out of here with blood streaming down both their legs — everyone in line turns around and goes back to their cars. They don't come back. And their friends don't come," she added.

Warnings

Despite the corn-rattler, despite fervent prayers, Chris admits that she can never predict what a group may or may not see, hear, or experience once she opens that gate. It is totally unpredictable. Yet, she has learned there are a couple of certainties that she always warns people about.

One warning Chris issues is to not take expensive cameras inside the cave. Electronic equipment goes haywire in there. Cameras malfunction, at best. At worse, cameras break completely.

"Sometimes on a tour, everyone's camera flashes start going off at the same time on their own," Chris said. "One man had his camera around his neck on a strap and his hands were in his pockets and the flash started going off repeatedly. It was blinding us all and everyone was shielding their eyes from it.

"The man said, 'That's weird. My camera is not even on. And the flash is off, too.' He finally had to take all of the batteries out to stop the flashes.

"I have also had many people to tell me that they took some pictures on a roll of film before they got here, while they were here, and after they left the farm. And when the photos were developed, all of the ones before and after turned out great. But all the pictures they took while here on our farm turned out black. Nothing at all is on them," she said.

Sometimes cameras work fine but will be blocked from taking a picture of a particular area of the cave.

"Someone can be snapping pictures in the cave and try to take a picture of one certain thing, like a crawlway or a flowstone and the camera will completely lock up," Chris said. "Then they will turn and snap a picture of something else and it will work fine, then turn back to take a picture of that certain crawlway or flowstone and it will lock up again. Once that happens, it's impossible to get a shot of it and the person will ultimately leave and not have a picture of it."

Chris' other warning entails far more serious ramifications than a malfunctioning camera. In fact, she cautions to circumvent bodily injury. Her warning: *Do not ever, ever taunt them — do not antagonize the spirits.*

"Occasionally, we get a loudmouth on a tour who's real obnoxious and yells things like, 'If you're so bad, bring it on!'

I always warn them not to do that, because sometimes — the spirits do bring it on," Chris said.

"Once a guy barely got the words out of his mouth when a bat came out of nowhere and dived straight into his head. He started yelling, trying to get out of the cave, plowing over everyone else. When we met up with him later in the parking lot, he was white as a ghost. He said, in no uncertain terms, the force in that cave is real," she added.

This Cave is Not for the Faint of Heart

The Kirbys have lived and worked on the Bell Witch Farm for more than a decade and that's a feat not many would be willing to undertake. No one knows that better than they do. When they bought the farm, they were shocked and saddened to discover that it cost them a few old friends who wanted nothing more to do with them because of it.

"When we told them that we had bought the Bell Witch Farm, most just looked at us weird then kind of cooled the friendship. They began avoiding us, not returning our phone calls. One of them actually became furious and started yelling at us," Chris recalled. "Like we had sold our souls to the devil, gone over to the dark side or something."

The first time this author entered the Bell Witch Cave was on a private tour given by Chris on an autumn afternoon. It was at dusk, just as the last customer was leaving and Walter was locking the gates out by the road.

We entered the cave with flashlights, cognizant of the sound of the Red River flowing peacefully below us, melodiously in tune to our own footsteps trekking along the pebbled floor of the cave.

But just a few feet inside the entrance, I was startled by a sudden powerful, rumbling noise which seemed to engulf us from all sides. I stopped dead in my tracks and looked toward Chris, hoping to see her nonchalant and blowing it off as a common experience — the way I search out the faces of flight attendants on turbulent flights, hoping to receive the cue that all is well. Instead, I found Chris wide-eyed and frozen in fear — as terrified as I was. It was in that moment that I understood.

The rest of the world is intrigued by this infamous haunting known as the Bell Witch. We range in attitude from cynical to curious possessing openness to the possibility — to true belief. The Kirbys don't believe. They know.

"I respect whatever it is," said Walter, a former member of the United States Armed Forces and high school linebacker. "Let's just say I'm not stupid enough to go down there and taunt it."

Living and working at the Bell Witch Farm and Cave can be compared to the lot of the lion tamer. Who knows the razor sharpness of the lion's claws and teeth more acutely than the owner? Who has more respect for its strength?

To know what could happen if things got out of hand, one needs only to look to former Bell Witch Farm owner, John Bell, who not only lost control — he lost his life.

*The Bells are now speaking
from the other side*

Chapter Twelve

Voices From The Past

How would immediate members of the Bell family feel about the new discoveries made possible through the use of twenty-first century technology? How would they react to the news that many spirits inhabit the land — that they had been living on top of a doorway to the spirit world?

They would probably feel vindicated. Aside from the mental, emotional and physical torture that it delivered, by all accounts, this infamous phenomenon was an embarrassment to the Bells. They viewed it as a stain on their good name.

Indeed, it is reported in various publications that some people of that time were convinced the Bell family must have done something to "deserve" their fate. One prevailing rumor even accused John Bell of murdering his neighbor, Kate Batts, and theorized that the "witch" was Kate's spirit getting her revenge. (In truth, Kate Batts lived for thirteen years beyond John Bell.)

Some people speculated that since the spirit followed daughter Betsy to the home of friends and neighbors where she went to escape the torture at home, she was the target and had somehow brought this grief upon her family.

Others were convinced the entire matter was a hoax, created by the family for financial gain, although they never made a cent off the haunting and, in fact, kept their "family troubles" a sworn secret until it became unbearable, forcing them to seek help from friends and neighbors.

As for how the Bells would view today's scientific documentation, we need only to turn to the pages of the old books where their voices, like those of the spirits, now speak from the other side.

> "At some time, it will be known what it is and I hope it will be understood."
> **— J.T. Bell, son of John Bell Jr.**

> "Though the world may not recognize spirits, whether good or demon, both will be here; it will have many of each."
> **— The Bell Witch**

Section III:

Bells' Hell

Then "it" came into the house

Chapter Thirteen

The Arrival

After moving from North Carolina to the frontier town of Adams, Tennessee (known then as Red River) in 1804, John and Lucy Bell had three more children, bringing the total to nine (seven sons and two daughters). The family quickly rose to prominence. They were active in the Red River Baptist Church and their farm — overlooking the river — was prime real estate. Their large one-and-a-half-story home, constructed of hewn logs, was considered to be one of the finest in the region. Also, in those days in the South, wealth was judged by the number of slaves a man had ... and John Bell was considered to be quite well-to-do.

The Bell children were Jesse, John Jr., Drewry, Benjamin, Esther, Zadok, Elizabeth (Betsy), Richard Williams and Joel Egbert. Esther, the oldest daughter, married Bennett Porter of Red River and moved out of the Bell home before the "family troubles" began.

The first indication that something was amiss on the farm came in 1817 with the mysterious appearance of several large animals, strange mutants belonging to no known breed. John spotted the first one sitting between two rows of corn, staring blankly into his eyes. At first glance, the creature appeared to be an enormous black dog. But as he drew closer, John realized that it was not a dog but a beast like no other he had ever seen.

Several days later, Drew observed what he thought was a

wild turkey perched on the fence at the edge of the yard. He quickly stepped inside to get his rifle but when he returned, he realized that it was not a turkey but a large breed of fowl he had never seen before — nor ever saw again. The bird stared vacantly at him, spread its wings and sailed off into the sky.

Soon after that, one of the slaves, Dean, reported seeing a large black dog on the property — which proceeded to vanish before his eyes.

These reports were only mildly perplexing to the Bell family. They had no idea that the weird incidents were mere precursors to the hell that was about to unfold.

Shortly after the appearance of the mutant animals, Betsy walked out to the edge of the yard along the tree line with her younger brothers where she spotted something in the treetops, which she described as a pretty little girl dressed in green, swinging from a top limb of a tall oak tree. As she drew closer, the girl vanished.

Following these peculiar sightings came a late-night rapping on the exterior walls of the home. The family was again not alarmed, assuming it was the work of pranksters.

Then "it" came into the house.

On a moonless Sunday night, the Bell sons were awakened by the sound of a large rat gnawing vigorously on a bedpost in their second-story bedroom. They jumped out of bed with the intention of killing it and the noise ceased. They lit a lamp and examined the bedpost but found no damage.

They returned to bed, only to hear the noise again. This time, they searched every inch of the room, finding no rat nor even a crevice by which a rat could enter. Yet every time they went back to bed, the noise resumed.

This series of events continued all night, then every night and week after week, eventually spilling over into the next room occupied by their sister, Betsy.

Betsy screamed each time the racket invaded her room, which would alarm her parents whose bedroom was on the first floor, sending them racing up the stairs.

Scratching and Gnawing

Soon the sounds of gnawing were accompanied by scratching noises on the wooden floors and banging on the walls which perpetually increased in force.

During the light of each day, a more thorough investigation was done throughout the house, turning over every stick of furniture, finding no trace of an animal nor any damage created by one.

Eventually, the family members stopped getting out of bed to conduct the futile searches, hoping they could learn to sleep despite the noises. That's when an unseen force started jerking their blankets off of them continuously and as fast as they could replace them. Then the sounds of lip-smacking accompanied by the peal of gnashing teeth filled the air.

"Then we heard a loud gulping sound," Williams writes in his diary. "Like someone choking or strangling. Some new performance was added nearly every night with all of the former ones continuing, and it troubled Betsy more than anyone else. Occasionally, the sound was like trace chains dragging and chairs falling over."

At other times, the noise grew deafeningly loud, sounding like horrific fights between dogs savagely chained together.

During the tirades, members of the family cried, screamed, and held on to each other — praying aloud for protection — crying out in the name of the Lord to deliver them from this evil. But nothing quieted the terror. When they demanded in the name of Jesus to know what it wanted, it responded with vicious laughter.

A side effect of the nightly terror was the sleep deprivation it forced upon all of them. They coped as well as they could by taking advantage of any and every opportunity to take a nap during the day. They began to retire early each evening, hoping to get in a few hours of peaceful sleep before the nightly trepidation began. That's when the physical attacks were launched against them.

'It Raised Me Off the Bed'

"I had just fallen into a sweet doze when I felt my hair beginning to twist," Williams writes. "And then with a sudden jerk, it raised me off the bed. It felt like the top of my head had been taken off."

Immediately, Joel screamed out in pain and terror, then Betsy. Up to this point, John and Lucy had instructed their children not to speak of the nightly perils to anyone outside the home. They were a proud independent farm family, determined to handle it themselves. They felt embarrassed, even shame, about the incomprehensible "difficulty" that was plaguing their home.

But after about a year of the terror steadily escalating, the whole house began to shake convulsively each night as if rocked by earthquakes. This violent shaking and intense noises could be seen and heard outside the home — a full half-mile down the road. Soon, John and Lucy realized that it was fruitless to try to hide their family troubles any longer and sought outside help themselves.

They confided in their closest neighbor and friend, James Johnson, who along with his wife, offered to spend the night in the Bell home to help them get to the bottom of the mysterious happenings.

Initially, the Bells suspected that nothing abnormal would occur when outsiders were in the home to witness it and that they might at least get a night's sleep. But they were dead wrong. "It" was alarmingly bold.

"Mr. Johnson was a devout Christian who read from the *Bible* and prayed fervently and earnestly for our deliverance from the frightful disturbance, or that its origin, cause and purpose might be revealed," Williams writes.

"But soon after everyone retired, the nightly disturbance commenced as usual: gnawing, scratching, knocking on the walls, overturning chairs, pulling the covers off of beds, etc. Every act was being exhibited as if on purpose to show Mr. Johnson what could be done, appearing in his room, as in other rooms. As soon as we lit a lamp and light would appear, the troubles would cease in that room and begin in another room.

"Mr. Johnson listened attentively to all of the sounds and capers, and that which appeared like someone sucking air through their teeth," Williams adds.

Then Johnson called out to it. "In the name of the Lord, what, or who are you? What do you want and why are you here?"

This silenced it for an hour or so but when it returned, it was more vigorous than ever, delivering blows to Betsy's face until her cheeks glowed crimson in the light of the lamp.

Johnson quickly determined that the situation was far beyond his scope of knowledge and ability and advised the Bells to seek additional help in solving this mystery.

With the Bells' consent, Johnson formed a committee comprised of the best minds in the region to conduct an investigation. The Bell family secret quickly spread throughout the community — and beyond.

*With little prompting, it revealed what it wanted:
"I've come to kill John Bell"*

Chapter Fourteen

The Spirit Speaks

Our neighbors were all touched with generous sympathy and were unremitting in their efforts to alleviate our distress," Williams writes. "It had become a calamity and people came every night to sit and watch with us."

And every night "it" performed its acts of terror upon the house and its occupants with no regard to the number of witnesses gathered. In fact, at times it seemed that the larger the audience, the larger the demonstrations.

By this time, the mystery had gained wide notoriety and people came from all over the country and eventually from around the world to witness these supernatural events. Rarely was anyone disappointed.

Curiosity-seekers who couldn't crowd into the house pitched tents on the front lawn where they watched as lights that looked similar to candles or lamps were routinely spotted flitting across the yard and through the fields. It was also common for stones and chunks of wood to fall, seemingly from the sky into the yard, as if hurled by an unseen force from above.

Many inside the house tried to communicate with the spirit, asking it such questions as how many people were in the room, to which the correct answer would come in raps or claw-like scrapings on the walls. Often, the most vocal person in the crowd would be pummeled with blows to the head as if coming from a fist that could be heard by everyone — but seen by no one.

After spiritual leaders, detectives and others persistently urged the spirit to communicate, it developed a whistle delivered in low broken tones as if it were trying to speak. This progressed to a weak whisper of indistinct words, gradually growing to a soft murmur that could be understood but only if the crowd remained totally silent.

Then it found a voice — a weird, distinctly feminine voice that seemed not to come from any one direction but rather as a disembodied voice freely roaming about the room.

A dozen people were present in the front room of the Bell home that night. Each sat totally still, afraid to even breathe, though their silhouettes oscillated on the walls from the flickering light of the fireplace.

"I am the spirit of a person who was once very happy, but have been disturbed and made unhappy," the voice said. "I am the spirit of a person who was buried in the woods nearby, and the grave has been disturbed, my bones disinterred and scattered." Then with little prompting, it revealed what it wanted. "I've come to kill John Bell," it said.

Everyone present was aghast. As word quickly spread that the spirit was actually speaking, more and more people came to hear the miraculous disembodied voice, which by now had been dubbed "the Bell Witch."

As implausible as it sounded, the Bells realized that the statement about bones being disinterred correlated to an incident that occurred on the farm several years earlier when farmhands discovered the mound of graves along the river, which they rightly assumed belonged to Native Americans.

Hoping to find relics buried with the dead, Drew Bell had opened one of the graves and proceeded to disinter the bones.

Finding no other relics, he brought the jawbone to the house. John reprimanded his son for his blatant disrespect for the dead and ordered him to return it to its grave — which he did.

The incident had all but been forgotten and seemed rather insignificant — until now.

One night when the Bell house was full of people who had come to hear the spirit speak (as it did each night now without fail), their neighbor, Calvin Johnson, began trying to talk the witch into shaking his hand. It consented but only after he had promised not to try to grab it. Johnson promised and held out his hand. The spirit placed its hand lengthwise on his so he could not grasp it but just feel it. He described it as small and feminine. This not only matched the voice they were hearing but the handprints left frequently across people's cheeks.

On countless nights, detectives, self-avowed conjurers and experts in divining mysteries visited the home and the family graciously, even anxiously, let them all try to solve the mystery. One such visitor had come from the East Coast, declaring that he was a witch killer who had a divine gift to see witches, which enabled him to shoot and kill them with silver bullets.

The man conjured around for several days with hairballs and foxfire, washing out his gun with a charm mixture, molding silver bullets and loading them into his gun, but the witch never showed.

The man concluded that the witch was afraid of him and would not appear as long as he was there. The Bells, having never been free of the witch for so many consecutive days, were beginning to believe the man was right and wanted to hire him to keep the witch away permanently. The man agreed to take the job but said he needed to return home to New England first to retrieve his belongings.

"But I suspect you will find in my absence that the witch is gone for good," the witch killer smugly declared. But when the man loaded his rations on his horse and attempted to ride away, his horse would not budge.

The man kicked the horse, spurred him, even whipped him; the horse reared up, bucked and fell down but was a no-go.

Suddenly, out of the clear sky, came the familiar tinny voice of the witch saying, "I can make that horse go. Let me get on behind."

With that, the horse darted off, seemingly of its own accord, making a circle around the yard, kicking and squealing in a wild rage and with the witch hollering, "Hold on, old man! Hold on!"

Finally, the horse struck a beeline for the gate and out he went, kicking and snorting, the rider hanging on to the mane of the horse's neck and yelling for dear life.

The witch laughed for a week over the escapade, claiming to have stuck the man full of brass pins on his way out. "He will spit brass pins for the next six months," it laughed. "But he will never come back here again." And he never did.

Bewildering Nonbelievers

One theme that played out in the Bell home (and still does in the Kirby home today) is the witch's love of bewildering nonbelievers, especially those who come to debunk the witch tales. According to Williams, it even followed some of them home, hounding them and inviting them back if they would like to try again to solve the mystery.

No one who ever visited the Bell home questioned that the power of the witch was real and that the phenomenon was beyond possible human trickery — at least, that's the way they felt by the time they left.

One of these instances involved two young men from Philadelphia who came to investigate, reportedly expecting to open the door of the Bell home and see the witch sitting there — as if it were human. However, after spending a disappointing afternoon waiting to at least hear the witch, one commented, "We are a pair of fools to make a trip like this on what some other sucker told us."

With that, the spirit spoke to them, immediately getting

down to business. "What do you gentlemen wish to see or hear?" it asked. "It would be of no value for me to tell you what is going on in your homes at this instant. You would not believe that. Suppose I tell you, as I have told other suckers, about your pasts?

"Do not look so frightened," the witch continued. "Neither one of you has been to jail. But you both went to a big Eastern school where your professor of philosophy was inclined to believe in spirits and certain mental states of human beings, which put his classes into deep thinking. Now, that is why you are here. To prove him wrong and to put him on the top of the sucker list."

The witch then called the professor's name and stated that he had died or he would most certainly have been there with them.

The men were bowled over, exclaiming that the witch was a hundred percent accurate. Then they began asking every scientifically-based question they could muster to try to solve the mystery — the miracle — that was speaking directly to them.

The men departed as true believers. However, they did not solve the mystery.

One scientist came from England. Though he stayed for months and witnessed a multitude of remarkable happenings, he remained quiet, reserved, thoughtful and did not express his opinions. So, the witch did it for him, reading his mind and repeating his thoughts out loud.

The witch discerned that he was intelligent to refrain from saying the foolish things that others had said. Then it vowed to perform some antics that would astonish him. It began informing him of things that were going on with his own family back in England. When letters came from home to him, the news that the witch had reported was always confirmed. Then it invited him to convey any message for his family and it would carry it to them.

The Englishman said, "Tell them that in my opinion,

never since the world was created have men seen and heard the marvelous things that I have witnessed during the past three months."

The Englishman's response from his family came within three hours and was delivered by the witch in the voices of his family members.

The voice of his mother said, "Tell him not to stay any longer. He has heard and seen enough and we do not want any more visits like this here!"

"Some who came to visit were detectives, confident of exposing the mystery," Williams writes. "Various opinions were formed and expressed. Some credited its own story and believed it was an Indian spirit. Some thought it was an evil spirit from Hell; others declared that it was witchcraft."

But they were all only unsubstantiated guesses. Not one of them could prove their theory nor definitively solve the mystery. Most poignantly, no one could alleviate the suffering of the Bell family.

The nightly tirades continued.

"It could quote any passage of scripture in the Bible from Genesis to Revelation"

Chapter Fifteen

Mimicking The Scriptures

Having launched its voice, the witch no longer contained its demonstrations to darkness and could be heard speaking openly in the light-of-day, often precisely mimicking the voices and words of others.

Church services were no exception. Although most of the people who settled in Robertson County considered themselves to be very religious, actual church buildings were scarce in the early days of settlement. So, midweek prayer services were commonly held in private homes, including the Bell home, though their neighbor James Johnson led the services. His was the first voice mimicked by the spirit.

When Johnson stood up before those gathered at the Bell home to begin his sermon, the spirit broke out in scripture, song and prayer, repeating every word that Johnson had uttered in the Bell home on the first night he and his wife had come to investigate their troubles. It was delivered with perfect impersonation.

"It could sing any song in the hymn book and quote any passage of scripture in the *Bible* from Genesis to Revelation," Williams writes. "If anyone misquoted a verse, they would be promptly corrected."

One Sunday night, two local preachers were in the Bell home, along with the usual crowd of spectators, when the witch began reciting the sermon that one of them had preached earlier in the day, word-for-word, mimicking his voice to a tee. When the preacher asked how it was able to do that, the spirit answered, "I was there."

The other preacher chuckled, saying that he was obviously off the hook for the night since his Sunday service was held at the exact same time of the morning, thirteen miles away ... until the witch began delivering his sermon, word-for-word, mimicking his voice to a tee.

"How did you do that?" they asked in disbelief. The witch's answer was the same, "I was there."

Eventually, the witch began to interrupt Sunday services at the church buildings, not only joining in the singing but even singing solo, posing spiritual songs that had never been heard before by anyone who witnessed it.

"Oh, Lordy, the devil has me by the nose"

Chapter Sixteen

A United States President And The Witch

Among the thousands who flocked to the Bell home to witness the extraordinary events, General Andrew Jackson (who later became the seventh president of the United States, 1829–1837) was the most celebrated.

Jackson, who lived approximately a hundred miles away, was already acquainted with the Bell family because their son, John Jr., had served with him in the Battle of New Orleans.

When Jackson heard all of the fantastic tales about events occurring at the Bell home, he had no intention of missing it. As one witness stated, "General Jackson's party came from Nashville on horseback, trailing a wagon loaded with a tent and provisions, bent on a good time and much fun investigating the witch." Among those with Jackson was a self-extolled "witch slayer" who armed himself with a large horse gun, loaded with a silver bullet.

All along their journey, the men in Jackson's party were devising plans for handling the witch if it pulled such stunts on them as it had on others.

As they neared the Bell home, traveling on a smooth, straight dirt road, the wagon suddenly came to a halt. The driver cracked his whip and the horses strained and pulled with all of their might but the wagon seemed to be fused to the road, as if welded to the earth.

Jackson commanded his men to dismount, to put their shoulders to the wagon's wheels and dislodge it. They did as instructed, pushing with all of their strength as the driver lay on his lash, spurring the horses to pull. But they could not budge it. Not one inch. Jackson then ordered that each wheel be removed from the wagon and examined. That was done and each wheel proved to be in perfect order. The wheels were then placed back on the wagon where each one was tested to spin freely on its axis.

They tried to move the wagon again, man and beast pushing and pulling together with determined force — and the wagon would not move. For no apparent reason, they were just plain stuck.

Exasperated, Jackson threw up his arms and exclaimed, "By the eternal, boys, it is the witch!"

Then came a strange metallic voice from the bushes saying, "All right, General. I will let the wagon move. I will see you again tonight."

The men immediately converged upon the bushes, fanning out to find the source of the voice, but found nothing. Then immediately, as if on cue, the horses took off drawing the wagon as smoothly as ever.

By the time Jackson's party reached the Bell farm, they were hellbent on retaliation and immediately formed search teams to find the source of their vex. Jackson went with them. In fact, he led them. But they found nothing.

That evening, they went into the house to sit and wait for the witch to make its nightly appearance.

The witch slayer, described as a brawny man with long black hair, a hawk-bill nose and fiery eyes, held a tight grip on his gun as he boasted about his alleged successes in witch slaying. This went on until the early hours of the morning as they continued to wait for the witch to come.

Finally, Jackson had heard all of the witch slayer's bragging he cared to hear. He leaned over to the man seated next to him and whispered, "I'll bet he's an errant coward. I do wish the thing would come. I want to see him run."

Immediately, a prancing sound was heard on the wooden floor in front of Jackson and then the same metallic voice he had heard earlier in the bushes said, "All right, General. I'm here and ready for business."

The voice then challenged the witch slayer.

"Here I am. Shoot!" The witch slayer pulled a severed cat's tail out of his coat pocket and rubbed it on his nose for luck. He then pointed his gun toward the voice and pulled the trigger but the gun failed to fire.

"Try again," the voice said. He pulled the trigger a second time but got the same result. Nothing.

"Now it's my turn, you old hypocrite fraud," the witch said. The next sounds heard were violent blows striking the man's face and head with such force that he tumbled over backward in his chair. The man scampered to his feet and began faltering around the room like a cowering dog. Then he cried out, "Oh, Lordy, the devil has me by the nose! He's pulling my nose off!"

At that moment, the front door flew open and the witch slayer charged out of it, screaming in pain, running across the yard. Everyone who was in the house ran outside, fearing they would find him dead or severely injured. But as far as they could see and hear, he was running up the lane, still screaming, "Oh, Lordy. Oh, Lordy."

As soon as the man was out of sight, Jackson abruptly collapsed to his knees. Everyone was horrified until they realized that his knees had buckled under the weight of his own laughter.

Jackson told Bell that he had never had such a tremendous laugh in his life and that he would like to camp on his lawn for an entire week.

However, after Jackson discussed the matter with the members of his party, they pulled out the next morning.

*"My name is Black Dog and you
split my head into two"*

Chapter Seventeen

The Witch And The Slaves

Woven throughout the tapestry of the old Bell Witch books are tales of the African-Americans who were held in slavery on the Bell farm — and their encounters with the witch. Though in most instances in Williams' diary his telling of these stories is nearly as racist as the act of owning a slave, the Kirbys wanted the stories recorded in this book.

"The slaves were here," Chris said. "We can't ignore that fact and we can't rewrite history."

(Note: The original language has been censored but readers are warned that these stories are told through the eyes of Williams who was born and raised in the thick of slavery and in all probability, as an adult, became a slave owner himself.)

The Slave Called Dean

According to Williams, the witch despised the Bells' slaves and (much to the slaves' relief) avoided their cabins. They were safe in their own homes. "But away from their quarters, they encountered a sight of trouble," he writes.

The slave known as Dean, or "Uncle Dean," had been with John and Lucy Bell since their wedding day in 1782. Dean and his mother, Chloe, were wedding gifts from Lucy's father, John Williams of Edgecombe County, North Carolina.

In fact, Dean had driven one of the large wagon teams that had taken the Bell family to Tennessee. As one Bell family member is quoted as saying about Dean, "He was Mr. Bell's most trustworthy servant and money could not buy him." Dean was also a confidant to John and was sometimes consulted on business decisions. His word was never questioned by anyone.

Dean frequently encountered the witch during his visits each night to his wife's cabin on the neighboring farm of Alex Gunn, although he always carried his ax and a "witch ball" made by his wife, Kate, for his protection. (Kate made the ball of hairs from her own head, yarn and various herbs.)

During some of his encounters with the witch, the entity appeared to him as a black dog — sometimes with two heads and at other times with no head at all.

According to Williams, Dean commonly showed up for work in the mornings with his head bloodied and bruised, saying that the witch had inflicted the wounds with a stick. Dean was no easy target. He was a large man whose prowess as a mighty rail-splitter was known throughout the region. Besides, Williams writes, "Under no circumstance would a Negro tell a lie on a ghost."

One particularly dark night, as Dean was en route to visit Kate, the witch stopped him, warning that it knew all about the witch ball he was hiding inside his coat. It then began taunting him about whether or not he thought it could actually protect him.

Trembling with fear, Dean dropped to his knees in prayer, begging the Lord Jesus to protect him.

The witch mocked his prayers ordering him to "Get up off of the ground, you fool, and give me that witch ball before I turn you into a stallion and ride you across the river to the stillhouse."

Dean reached into his coat, pulled out the ball and held it out in the direction of the voice for the witch to take. The ball suddenly burst into flames in his hands and then blasted into the sky like a shooting star.

Dean was struck dumb, unable to move, until he suddenly became aware that the witch had taken the form of the ominous black dog who was at his side, laughing wildly at him.

Enraged, Dean picked up his ax, reared it back over his shoulder and, with one powerful blow, split the dog's head wide open, ensconcing the head of his ax so deeply into the ground that it disappeared. With that, he took off running to the safety of his wife's cabin.

Kate nursed him back from a state of shock and proceeded to make him a more potent witch ball. This time, instead of using a potion from her own African heritage, she used a Native American formula that her father assured her would be more effective against this particular aberration. Kate's father, who was called "Uncle Zeke," also lived on the plantation of Alex Gunn and had consulted a Native American in the area to obtain the witch ball recipe. But the old Indian had issued a warning about the formula that was passed along to Dean: "Whoever lets this witch ball fall into the hands of a witch would anger the gods and would instantly be struck dead."

Still, the new and improved witch ball did little to deflect trouble. In fact, Dean swore that the next time he saw that dog on his way to Kate's house — and from then on — it had two heads.

"When I first saw it standing there on the trail with two heads, I stopped dead in my tracks and said, 'In the name of the Lord, what's that?' And it grinned at me with both mouths, showing me two sets of big white teeth. Then it said, 'My name is Black Dog and you know me. You split my head into two,'" Dean said.

The dog then demanded Dean's new witch ball. But this time, Dean denied having one and began backing away from the dog, farther and farther until the dog was no longer in sight. However, when he spun around to dart back the other way, there stood the dog, grinning at him with both sets of sharp teeth.

"I didn't want to be struck dead by the gods for letting it have the witch ball, so I had no choice but to fight," Dean recalled in his later years. "I told the dog I was going to take my ax and split him open down to his tail this time."

But before Dean could lift up his ax, he felt a spell being cast over him. "Say your prayers, Dean," he heard the dog growl as he suddenly became too weak to stand. Dean then found himself locked in a precarious state, bent over at the waist with both hands and both feet on the ground, bearing the stance of a mule.

Then, out of the darkness, he heard two female voices discussing the feasibility of riding him. One voice complained that "He's too high to double-tote." Then the pair began to argue about which witch would ride and which witch would lead.

Finally, Dean felt the weight of one witch mounting his back, declaring that they would ride to Hell for breakfast, while the other witch grabbed hold of his ear and began to lead.

"I tucked my head down low and raised both of my legs up over my back and kicked with all my might," Dean recalled. "Then I saw two witches go flying over the fence into the field, so I tore off down the lane on all fours to Kate's cabin."

When he reached the cabin, Dean could not open the door or even knock on it. He was reduced to pawing at it and finally managed to pry it open.

As soon as the door swung open and he saw sweet Kate sitting by the light of the fire mending his clothes, the love he felt for her instantly dispelled the hex and he was able to stand upright again.

Dean lived to be quite elderly and, in his later years, the children of Robertson County (Black and White) would gather around him to hear his tales of the Bell Witch. Although he carried a large scar on his forehead that he vowed came from a gash inflicted by the witch, he was able to joke about some of his encounters with the demon.

"The night I heard those witches talking about riding me to Hell for breakfast, I was the most scared mule you've ever seen," he said. "I imagine it's a rocky road to Hell and I wouldn't know how to get back. Besides, I was in my rail-splitting clothes and I would have felt bad around all those finely dressed gentlemen down there."

Dean also talked about the witch attending the slaves' baptisms that took place at the mouth of Sturgeon Creek, which empties into the Red River just north of the Bell farm.

Whenever the spirit arrived, the slaves would panic and start to scatter. But the witch commanded them to stay, threatening to drown them in the creek if they tried to flee.

Often, the witch joined in singing the hymns and when someone known as a real sinner was baptized, it would yell, "Parson, you had better put him under again and keep him there a little longer."

Harry the Houseboy

Harry, the Bells' young houseboy, was pummeled by the witch on numerous occasions. "It was Harry's business to make the morning fires before daylight," Williams writes. "He became negligent in this duty and Father scolded and threatened him several times."

But Harry continued to be late. Finally, one morning, he was later than ever. He went into the house, laid the kindling wood down, and was on his knees blowing on the coals, trying to get them to blaze when an unseen force attacked him.

John heard the blows which sounded like they came from a paddle or a strip of wood, being meted out against the boy with full force and he could hear Harry screaming for his life but could see nothing. "Harry the Houseboy was never late after that," Williams writes.

Phillis

Phillis was a young African-American girl who assisted her mother, known as "Aunt Lucy," in the kitchen.

One day, a log-rolling was held on the Bell farm. As was customary in the day among the farm owners, a log-rolling was a way to make a party out of the work that needed to be done, while garnering help from their neighbors.

After the work was finished, the youngsters from the neighboring farms engaged in some gymnastic exercises, attempting to bring their legs up in front of their own chests and lock their heels behind their heads.

Phillis, who was twelve, observed these exercises and the next day she stole away upstairs to be alone and test her own athletic ability. After she tried unsuccessfully several times to get her feet up behind her head, suddenly they were forced behind her head and held there by an invisible energy, rendering her unable to move.

Needing Phillis' help in the kitchen, Aunt Lucy called out repeatedly to her before finally picking up a switch and heading up the stairs to get her.

According to Williams, "There was a racket upstairs and Aunt Lucy had worn the switch out on Phillis' rear end before she could explain that the witch had her."

*Betsy's presence was delivering torment to
the homes of all who reached out to try and help*

Chapter Eighteen

The Torment Of Betsy Bell

Though the Bells had nine children, the one child singled out for torment was their youngest daughter, a beautiful blonde named Betsy. She was only twelve years old when the horror started.

In the beginning, the thing would enter Betsy's room at night and slap her repeatedly until her cheeks were red and swollen. Her hair was pulled and she was racked by sharp pains over her entire body. She described the torture as feeling like pins were being inserted into her skin.

Then she began suffering seizures characterized by shortness of breath and smothering sensations. She would pant heavily, struggling for life itself, becoming entirely exhausted and lifeless. She would lose her breath for nearly a minute between gasps and was ultimately rendered unconscious. She would then come to for a moment, only to suffer the cycle again. These episodes lasted thirty to forty minutes and were ever-increasing in frequency.

Yet the timing of Betsy's spells wasn't random. They struck at the witching hour — just after the witch appeared in the evening and began its nightly talk, entertaining those who gathered at the Bell home. Strangely, while Betsy's spells were playing out, the witch was silent and remained so until after it had passed.

The silence of the witch during Betsy's spells caused some to speculate that young Betsy may have been responsible for the voice of the witch that she carried out through ventriloquism. However, those closest to the Bell family knew that the witch's silence during those times only proved that the witch was preoccupied — inflicting the spells on Betsy. Plus, the witch's antics occurred in the Bell home whether Betsy was there or not.

When it became obvious that the nightly outbursts were targeting John most severely and then Betsy, her parents packed her off to spend the night with sympathetic neighbors, hoping she could derive a peaceful night's sleep. But to the utter horror of her hosts, the brutalization followed her wherever she went.

Yet, at the same time, the nightly persecution at the Bell home never missed a beat. This obvious mobility of the spirit dissuaded the family from trying to flee the region, coupled with its steadfast promise to follow.

In Betsy's Own Words

For his publication in 1934, Dr. Charles Bailey Bell used an interview that he had conducted with Betsy many years earlier. Although Betsy was elderly at the time, her memory of the monstrous torture was acutely clear. Following are some of the accounts ... in her own words.

"When the spirit became so tantalizing, filling my mind with horror and causing me to become so nervous, my parents often sent me to a neighbor's house to rest for a night. My first night away from home was spent with Theny Thorn, one of my best girlfriends.

"Nothing was heard until after we retired, which we did early. We locked the door to our room securely. Just as soon as we had retired, there came a loud knocking on our outside door, which seemed to fly open and a great gust of wind was felt. Then our bed quilts were snatched off. Theny sprang up at once and lit a candle; to our surprise the door was not open. We adjusted the bedclothes and laid down again.

"Then a voice spoke very softly saying, 'Betsy, you should not have come over here; you know I can follow you anywhere. Now get a good night's sleep.' A soft hand patted my cheek and the voice again assured us that we would not be disturbed anymore that night.

"We both were very much excited [frightened], but we laid quite still and after so long a time fell asleep. The next day, Theny went home with me and my mother related that the spirit had told her all about our experience and for her not to be alarmed, that we would rest well and be home the next day," Betsy recalled.

Miracle in the Cave

In one of the few instances that the cave is mentioned in any of the old Bell Witch books, Charles Bailey Bell's book gives Betsy's description of it — and the miracle that occurred in it. Like the previous description about her night spent at the home of Theny Thorn, the story was recorded during Betsy's later years.

"On the river, near the north boundary of the farm, is a cave in the bluff, which is about three hundred feet high. There is sufficient room at the front of the cave for people to have lunches. Below the cave, the river makes a good fishing place and we often fished there.

"The cave became famous as the Bell Witch Cave. None of us ever knew of the cave being occupied by the spirit, but on our pleasure trips, we always heard its voice on the river or in the cave," Betsy said.

"There were beautiful stalactites in the cave. We often took candles and went back quite a way to a big room some thirty feet high with a kind of upstairs to it. After passing through this, the passage became small.

"One time when we were exploring the cave, one of the boys

in the crowd came to a place where he had to get down on his knees and crawl. He got into a kind of quicksand deposit and soon became so jammed in, he could not get out. His candle was out and no one could get to him. Suddenly, the big room and all parts of the cave were lit up as if by a big lamp. A voice called out, 'I'll get you out.' The boy's legs were then seized, as if by strong hands, and he was drawn out with a face full of mud that had nearly suffocated him," Betsy recalled.

"We all agreed not to tell our parents anything about this nearly fatal accident, but that night when the spirit arrived at the usual neighborhood gatherings at our home, it asked the boy's parents if they had gotten the mud out of his ears. Then it told them about his predicament earlier that day and advised them to put a halter on him, so his companions could pull him out if he got stuck again," she added.

The Force No One Could Repress

Few of Betsy's recollections of the witch were as gracious as the night it granted her a full night's sleep or rescued her friend from quicksand. For the most part, she recounted stories of heinous torture. One story in particular centered around a neighbor, Frank Miles, and his efforts to defend her from the evil.

"Of all our friends, none was thought of more highly than Frank Miles. Brother John and he would have died for each other without hesitation. The treatment the spirit gave me was resented as much by Frank as by my brother," Betsy said.

"As was well known, Frank was the most powerful man any of us ever saw and just as fearless as any living man. He was very tenderhearted and one time he said to me, 'Come, sit by me, little sister. I have come to give you a good rest. Nothing will bother you while I'm here.'

"This seemed to exasperate the spirit. It screamed, 'You go home; you can do no good here.' It then gave my hair such a jerk that my combs fell on the floor and it pinched my cheeks until they were red and ached.

"Frank fairly shook the house stomping on the floor and he dared it to assume any shape so he could get a hold of it. He went into such a rage that he swore terribly. (And I had never heard him curse before.) The scene was terrifying, as the spirit kept screaming at him to mind his own affairs. It told him that it had slapped him over before and to be careful or it would knock his block off.

"Frank apologized to me, patted my cheek and talked softly to me, telling the spirit that it was the biggest coward ever to visit this earth to torture a child, little more than a baby. Then he yelled, 'Why not work on me, you fiend of Hell?'

"Frank soon learned that it was of no avail to offer to champion me in a fight; it only made matters worse," she added.

Other friends and neighbors tried in vain to relieve Betsy's torment. Several threw social functions in their homes to steal her away for a few hours so then she could enjoy a normal teenage life. Some gave fishing parties on the bank of the river. She even went to live with relatives in Kentucky for a time but the witch followed her wherever she went.

Facing the fact that her presence was delivering torment to the homes of all who reached out to try and help and that she was becoming an unwelcome visitor in anyone's home, Betsy began to withdraw, leaving the Bell farm less and less frequently.

In spite of its reign of terror which initially lasted four years (throughout her puberty), Betsy grew into a lovely young woman but she did not emerge unscathed.

By the time she was sixteen, the fiend had taken her father's life, her health ... and the love of her life.

*The Bell Witch had a hand in
Betsy's misery until the day she died*

Chapter Nineteen

Lost Love

Betsy Bell and Joshua Gardner had been friends since childhood and when they became teenagers, their friendship caught fire, forming a deep bond of love.

Classically handsome, Joshua was tall with black hair and soft gray eyes, and he came from a well-respected family. Though he was quite familiar with the Bells' predicament, which was legendary by then, and despite the fact that many in the area had begun to stay away from the Bell farm, Joshua was headstrong and determined to be near her. He visited frequently and they became engaged.

Still unrelenting in its persecution of Betsy, the spirit continually harassed her in front of Joshua. Although Williams did not repeat in his diary what the spirit said to the young couple (as few would have in that day), he described the comments as being embarrassing, "personal in nature, causing Betsy to blush."

Then the spirit conjured up a new mission: to break up this love affair.

One balmy March day when Joshua was visiting Betsy, the couple slipped away for some quiet moments alone. They were sitting in the shade of a pear tree when it became apparent that they were not alone. They began hearing soft melancholy sighs in the distance which gradually approached nearer with gentle whispers "Please Betsy Bell, don't marry

Joshua Gardner. That would surely bring you a life of pain and misery."

Days, weeks and months went by with the spirit repeating the plea over and over in such beseeching and supplicating tones that it caused shudders to creep over everyone who heard it. (One has to wonder how the witch could be so concerned about Betsy's happiness when it was causing her life to be a living Hell.)

Joshua refused to be chased away from the love of his life by a fiend but Betsy's torture was being intensified during the nightly tirades. Her fearful convulsions escalated. Her breath was being suppressed by an increasingly greater force until the very life was almost extinguished from her. Throughout each night, the sound of Betsy's frantic screams was enmeshed in the sound of the witch's evil laughter and vile threats.

Still, it wasn't until the witch succeeded in putting her father in his grave that Betsy lost all hope and called off her impending marriage.

The Ultimate Cruelty

Three years after ending her engagement to Joshua, Betsy married her former schoolteacher, Richard Powell, who was eleven years her senior. They had a houseful of children and she was never bothered by the spirit again. Betsy's seizures completely ceased and she lived to the age of 82.

So it appears that the spirit was right — Betsy's life was happy without Joshua Gardner in it, right? Not so fast.

Betsy had an incredible amount of misery in her life. In fact, she had so much hardship and sorrow that one has to wonder how it could have been any worse if she had married Joshua.

We also have to wonder if the spirit knew that Betsy's life with Richard (not Joshua) would be miserable and deliberately led her down that painful path. In essence, although the witch was no longer making active appearances in Betsy's life, by rescripting her destiny, the Bell Witch had a hand in her misery until the day she died.

Betsy's Misery Included:

- Overwhelming grief: Betsy buried six of her eight children. Four of them died when they were small due to various accidents and illnesses. Of the four children who lived to adulthood, one was killed in the Civil War while he was still a young man. Another son died shortly after the war. Only two of her children lived to be middle-aged.

- Financial despair: While still a relatively young man, Betsy's husband suffered a stroke that left him permanently disabled and incapable of providing for his family.

- Betsy and Richard invested their life savings in a cargo shipment to New Orleans. The ship overturned and sank to the bottom of the river. They never recovered financially and spent the rest of their lives in poverty.

- In addition to burying six of her children, Betsy buried her husband, both of her parents and seven of her eight siblings.

- She was a widow for more than thirty years, suffering from grief, loneliness, poverty and morbid obesity.

The witch exhibited human-like emotion and compassion

Chapter Twenty

The Good Witch

As contemptible as the witch's treatment was toward Betsy and her father, it was as mercifully kind to her mother, Lucy.

"Old Luce is a good woman," the spirit frequently said. Although Lucy feared the thing and detested the harm that it was inflicting upon her family, she spoke kindly to it and about it, hoping to pacify it — hoping to keep it calm and to gain influence over its actions.

"This proved to be the best policy, for it is evident that she appeased its malice in many instances," Williams writes. "Except in father's case, toward whom the malignity was brutal, unrelenting and beyond control."

In September 1820, Lucy was stricken with life-threatening pleurisy. The witch's reaction to her illness was intriguing as it exhibited human-like emotion and compassion.

"Luce, poor Luce. I am so sorry you are sick," it kept saying. "Don't you feel better, Luce? What can I do for you, Luce?"

As the disease progressed, family members, friends and neighbors were constantly in and out of Lucy's room. But not the spirit. It remained with her around the clock. When anything was wanted or needed for Lucy's comfort, the witch would speak promptly, telling precisely where the article could be found. And so the strange voice continued in the room daily, mystifying everyone who came to visit. Though it was utterly impossible to distinguish from where the voice came, it was so pathetic that everyone who heard it found themselves feeling sympathy for it.

Still, Lucy's condition worsened and she eventually stopped eating. One day, as several neighborhood women were sitting by her bed, a handful of hazelnuts were dropped from above the bed, seemingly out of thin air and into Lucy's hands. At the spirit's urging, Lucy ate the nuts. Next came grapes, which were delivered in the same manner.

The startled women searched the second floor of the house directly above the bed and beyond, determined to find a loose plank or some kind of opening through which the nuts and grapes were dropped but they found nothing.

Soon afterward, Lucy regained her health and the household was back to "normal" with the witch's prattle entertaining everyone who came to the house each evening.

However, the action that the spirit had taken in manifesting the nuts and grapes would prove significant — far beyond nursing Lucy back to health. For the first time, the witch was able to go beyond moving tangible objects from one place to another to actually making things appear, seemingly out of nowhere. This newfound capability would put the last nail in her husband's coffin.

*"I've got him this time; he will
never get up from that bed again"*

Chapter Twenty-One

The Mysterious Death Of John Bell

The venomous abuse that the spirit heaped upon John at every level: physical, mental and emotional on a regular basis, both day and night for years would have taken its toll on any man. As his health disintegrated, John and his family became resigned to his fate, that the spirit was slowly, but surely killing him. There was no escape.

What they didn't expect, however, was that the spirit would take direct action in his murder.

After the spirit's last attack had left him beside the road in convulsions (during his walk to the hog pen with Williams) John never left the house again. For weeks, he was able to get out of bed for short periods but his health gradually declined. Eventually, he became an invalid, totally confined to his bed.

Lucy was constantly at his bedside while John Jr. consulted with the physician and administered his father's medications.

Meanwhile, the witch was unrelenting in its cruel tirades, reveling gleefully in its success as John held on for life.

On the morning of December 19, 1820, John did not awaken at his usual time and his family found him in a deep stupor. He could barely be aroused.

John Jr. went to the cupboard to get his father's prescribed medications but found that they had vanished. In their place was an ominous-looking smoky vial which was one-third filled with a dark liquid.

He immediately called every member of the family into the room, demanding to know where the prescriptions were and what the vial of smoky liquid was doing in the cupboard.

No one knew where the medicines were and no one had ever seen the mysterious vial of liquid before.

They immediately sent for Dr. George Hopson of the nearby Port Royal community. Neighbors John Johnston, Alex Gunn and Frank Miles were also summoned.

"Dr. Hopson was the only one who brought medicine into the house and it was handled very carefully," Williams writes. When he arrived, the doctor confirmed that he had not left the vial there. He smelled it but couldn't tell what it was.

At that moment, the witch stepped forward to take the credit saying, "It's useless for you to try to revive Old Jack. I've got him this time; he will never get up from that bed again. I put that vial there and I gave Old Jack a big dose of it last night while he was asleep. I fixed him. I fixed him."

Hopson bent down over John and smelled the same mysterious odor on his breath that was emitting from the bottle. He sunk into the chair by the bed in defeat, lamenting the fact that medical school had not prepared him for anything like this. Then he seemed to say a silent prayer before rubbing his eyes, regaining his composure and stepping back into the role of physician.

"We need to test it to see if it is indeed poison," Hopson said. With that, John Jr. yanked a piece of straw from a broom that was standing in the corner of the room. He slid the straw down the neck of the vial, coating the end of it with the black liquid. Then he picked up a gray cat from the kitchen floor and inserted the straw into its mouth, wiping the liquid across its tongue. The cat died instantly.

In a fit of rage, John Jr. picked up the vial and slammed it into the burning fireplace. It burst into an abominable purple smoke and quickly rose up the chimney.

His father never regained consciousness but labored to breathe throughout the day and night. He died the next morning.

No one heard a word from the spirit for the next few days as John's body laid in a coffin in the parlor of his home — pathetically defeated — just as the witch had promised. Yet at the same time, comfort came over the family with the knowledge that his torment was finally over. He was at peace.

Why the spirit stayed away in its grandest hour of victory is unknown, just as it had mysteriously vanished during Betsy's seizures. Perhaps it was because of its affection for Lucy — maybe it knew its presence during the worst moments of her life would be too unbearable for her.

However, after the funeral, as the dirt was being shoveled into John's grave, the spirit thrust itself onto the scene. In the words of Williams Bell, "It was a bright December day and a great crowd of people came to attend the funeral. And when they turned to leave the sad graveside scene, the witch broke out in a loud voice, singing, 'Row me up some brandy O. For on a journey I will go,' and continued singing this until the family and friends had all entered the house."

Lucy continued to live in the Bell family home for the remainder of her life. After John's death, the fury of the witch was greatly abated.

When Lucy died, the house stood vacant for many years and was eventually torn down.

The cave, the ominous cave, remains just as it was ....

Section IV:

Skeletons In The Closet

John Bell's desires were undeniably for twelve year old girls — he married one

Chapter Twenty-Two

The Author's Views

While this author believes that the "what" and the "why" of the Bell Witch haunting have been proven — as much as the supernatural can be proven — the Bell family phenomenon, in a sense, remains a mystery in its own right. Although this author has her opinions about that, they do not reflect those of the Kirby family.

So Many Questions Linger

- Why did the dominant spirit known as the Bell Witch hate John so vehemently — enough to put him in his grave?

- Out of the nine Bell children, why did it single out Betsy for torture and abuse?

- Why did the spirit treat Lucy Bell with such kindness?

This author concurs with the views portrayed in the movie *An American Haunting:* John was sexually molesting Betsy. Here is why the theory merits thought:

- It can certainly be argued that John's sexual appetite was bent toward twelve year old girls since he was thirty-two when he took Lucy for his wife, and she was twelve.

- The spirit did not come until the Bells' older daughter, Esther, married and moved out of the house which left Betsy alone in her own bedroom.

- Betsy was beautiful. The spirit arrived when she was twelve and stayed until shortly after her father died when she was sixteen. Why?

- Young girls who are victimized by incest are predisposed to poltergeist activity and, ironically, the incest victim herself is typically a target of the haunting.

- John was the most tortured member of the family, followed by Betsy, while Lucy (the poor betrayed wife) was doted on by the fiend.

- The spirit demonstrated no strong feelings at all toward the other members of the Bell family — good or bad. The key players were clearly the triangle of John, Betsy, and Lucy.

- According to the old Bell books, the spirit *did* state the reason why it was torturing John but that reason was never disclosed in the books. Why not? It is simply stated that the spirit was lying. (Remember, nothing came out of the Bell house except that which was brought out by a family member or someone close to the family. Therefore, all of our information about what went on in that home was subject to spin doctoring.) I believe that the spirit was stating repeatedly that it was torturing John because he was molesting Betsy.

- In his 1997 novel, *The Bell Witch*, author Brent Monahan alleges that Betsy poisoned her father and that this truth came out when her husband put her under hypnosis years later. I don't know about the hypnosis and I don't know who was guilty of causing John's death by poison. But I do know if homicide detectives were investigating the murder today, you had better come up with a story more convincing than "the witch did it."

It is also interesting that the neurological disorders John suffered from for two years prior to his death are consistent with a slow gradual poisoning. I do not believe that his death by poison was sudden.

A slow poisoning might also explain Betsy's mysterious neurological illness which, incidentally, vanished immediately after her father's death. Could the tortured young woman have been poisoning herself along with her father? Could Lucy, another member of the Bell family or one of the slaves, have been keen to what was going on and in order to stop the molestation — and the haunting — malevolently committed the poisoning(s)?

The Kirbys do not buy into the incest theory and are researching other possible explanations for the spirit's hatred of John.

"I think the incredibly strong spirit (that became known as the Bell Witch) was already here before the Bells came and it wanted them off the property," Chris said. "I think it attacked John the most severely because he was the leader of the family. And I think it attacked Betsy second because that was another way to get at John. What would be more painful to a parent, than to witness your beautiful, innocent child being abused?"

Personally, this author does not think that the mystery of why John and Betsy were singled out for torture will ever be proven. But, then again, I never would have dreamed that the

Kirbys, with help from anthropologists, archaeologists, historians and leaders in the field of paranormal phenomena, could have uncovered the truth behind the infamous haunting of the Bell Witch Cave.

Along with all the ghouls ... there were a few skeletons in the Bell family closet

Chapter Twenty-Three

What No One Wanted You To Know

There are facts about the Bell family that no one wanted you to know — at least no one who authored any of the original Bell Witch books. These are facts that the old books hedge and twist.

However, the Kirbys' research into the Bell family, based on church records, county land deeds, and other legal documents, uncovered some facts that would have raised a few eyebrows in the day. Yes, in addition to everything else they had to deal with, there were a few skeletons in the Bell family closet.

The Kirbys' Research Confirms:

- John killed a man in North Carolina before moving to Tennessee. The death was determined to be self-defense or justifiable homicide.

- John was excommunicated from the Red River Baptist Church. Church records show that he was kicked out when it was proven to the board of elders that he had charged a neighbor exorbitant interest rates on the rental of a slave.

- Kate Batts, the woman so often accused of being the Bell Witch or of conjuring up the witch, who was virtually shunned by the community — was, in fact, Lucy's niece. (Kate's father was Lucy's older brother.) While there are numerous references to Kate in the original Bell books, the fact that she was a blood relative is painstakingly omitted.

- It's also interesting to note that in those days, Native Americans were looked upon (by Whites) with little more esteem than the African-Americans held in slavery. Although the Kirbys have not been able to substantiate it, they believe that Kate and Lucy were of Native American descent. If that is true, these two proper "White" ladies were, in essence, "passing."

- As revealed in the previous chapter, John was thirty-two years old when he married Lucy ... and she was twelve. By today's laws, the man was a pedophile who should have gone to prison. He would have been forbidden to reside in the home with his beautiful twelve-year-old daughter.

Chapter Twenty-Four

Predictions Of The Bell Witch

The entity known as the Bell Witch departed shortly after the death of John Bell, vowing to make another visit in seven years. It did as promised, returning in March 1828, imparting various predictions to John Bell Jr. regarding the future of the United States and the world at large.

All of the witch's predictions have now come to pass — except one — and that is for the total destruction of the earth by fire. (Many people today believe that this bleak prediction foretells the imminent doom of nuclear war.)

Ironically, since the mission of the witch's first visit was one of evil and darkness — to torture a man to death — its second visit, it claimed, was to avail as a beacon of light and to save the world from destruction. The witch warned repeatedly and emphatically that the hope of the world can only be found in Christ-like love and light.

When John Jr. questioned the abrupt reversal of its mission, the witch replied, "There is a reason for my appearance here again, and if you will think with the thinking power of which you are capable, you will understand. On my first visit here, people thought the things I did were most unheard of and not of value; the very fact that I could talk was a wonder to them. What I am telling now is no greater wonder than things people thought of me when I was here before, but the vast importance of what is being told to you will seem incredible when given to the world."

The following predictions, conveyed to John Jr. in 1828, were recorded and published by his grandson, Charles Bailey Bell. They are validated by the fact that they were published in Bell's book in 1935, foretelling the United States' involvement in World War II, even though the war did not come to pass until 1941, six years after the predictions were published.

Bell Witch Predictions

- ### The Civil War

"The darkest hour in the history of the United States will come when the nation divides, causing brother to go to war against brother. But the result of the war will be the freedom of the Negro slaves," the witch said.

During this revelation, the witch talked to John Jr. about the Battle of New Orleans that he had helped to win during the War of 1812 under the command of General Andrew Jackson. The witch told him that New Orleans would be the turning point of the war between the North and the South — that the South would lose the city and, as a result, lose the war.

It also predicted that the fall of New Orleans would come at the hands of another Tennessean who would be fighting on the other side. "He is an officer in the U.S. Navy now," the witch said.

Historic Fact: New Orleans did fall at the hands of another Tennessean, David Glasgow Farragut. The witch was also correct in saying he was an officer in the U.S. Navy at the time of its visit. The city surrendered to him on April 24, 1862. This siege marked the end of the Civil War.

- **World War I**

    A great war, which will likely involve nearly the whole world, will occur. The U.S., at that time, will have become one of the world's greatest nations and will be drawn into this terrible struggle. Countries will be left in financial straits and years of suffering will invade every nation.

- **The Great Depression**

    As a result of the great war, the United States will suffer morally, financially, spiritually and thousands actually will suffer from want of the necessities of life.

- **World War II**

    The next war will be far more devastating and fearful in character than the one that the world thought was too terrible for the mind to grasp.

- **The U.S. Becomes a Superpower**

    The witch compared the enormous power that the United States would realize to that of the ancient Roman Empire and implored this new superpower to heed the lessons of history.

    It said that Rome fell because the government rejected Jesus Christ and that Christians prevail in Rome today.

    The spirit warned that the leaders of the United States would face great tests and trials, equal to those once faced by the Roman Empire and that if they were not properly handled, the country will become inundated with greed, meanness and oppression of the poor. The American middle class will be obliterated, leaving only the wealthy and the poor. "I shall be there at that time; there will be thousands of spirits unrecognized," it said.

As to whether the United States endures — or falls — is not predestined. The witch said that the outcome will be determined by the thoughts and actions of its people. "Will its people accept love, light, compassion and tolerance for their fellow man?" it asked. "Or will they adhere to greed, hate and oppression?"

- **The Lost Continent of Atlantis (and Other Great Civilizations)**

If scientists will dig under the right parts of the earth's surface, they will find the remains of a destroyed civilization from hundreds of thousands of years ago, the witch said.

"Where your farm is now, was covered by the sea; where the sea is now, once was land and a civilization — all gone, destroyed millions of years ago."

The witch stated that shifts in the earth's surfaces and oceans were created by earthquakes, sent by God to destroy with water the civilizations that had become greatly advanced in technology but whose people had become morally corrupt. It noted one such continent that boasted scientific advancements that towered over all others. (Most are convinced that this was a reference to Atlantis.)

What is now known as the United States of America was inhabited millions of years ago by a superior race, it stated. They were destroyed only to be succeeded by others. They underwent the hardships and struggles of building a great civilization. They had the wonderful buildings, great schools and mighty machinery that this era will acquire before it passes.

The Spirit not only spoke of past destructions of other continents — but of other worlds.

- **Destruction of the Planet Earth**

   The witch said while portions of the earth were capable of being inhabited after the great flood, the next destruction of Earth's civilizations will come by fire, rendering it uninhabitable. The witch also maintained that it did not base its prediction on the *Bible* as it states in the Book of Revelation. Rather it is based on its own observation of the fates of other worlds over the course of millions of years.

   "The people of this earth must not forget that this world will surely come to an end. The world can be destroyed by its Creator at any time or by any means that He chooses to bring the world of sinners to their knees. Its destruction can be complete within a few minutes.

   "At no time will the inhabitants of the world, as a whole, believe there will be an end to the world. At the time when they think least of it, the end will come. Worlds many times larger than this have been destroyed so suddenly that it was only like a powder-pan flash. Do not for one instant doubt what is being told to you," it said. "There will come a time when there will be more intelligence on this earth and all of this will be proven."

   The witch told John Jr. to pass on the things that it said to him, even though they seemed incredulous in 1828.

- **In The Last Days**

   Christians will put their money into elaborate church buildings rather than using that money to aid the poor — and helping the poor would have carried far greater favor in the eyes of the All Mighty. While righteous Christians will exist in the last days, the majority purporting to be Christians will be selfish, giving no thought to others, the witch said.

- **Longevity**

In the last days, people will live longer than they ever have but the world will have become so enlightened that there will be no more inventions worth having, it added.

- **Is There Hope For The World?**

Even with its grim prophecy for the end of civilization, the witch declared that there is hope and it avowed itself a messenger who could avert destruction of the world.

"But when you see the poor become helpless and starving, the rich thinking only of themselves, and suffering becomes so widespread all over the world that the Creator will no longer permit it, then prepare for ...

... The End

www.ingramcontent.com/pod-product-compliance
Lightning Source LLC
Chambersburg PA
CBHW051451290426
44109CB00016B/1715